ANTIGUA AND BARBUDA

The heart of the Caribbean

ANTIGUA AND BARBUDA

The heart of the Caribbean

Brian Dyde

MACMILLAN CARIBBEAN

First published 1986
Reprinted 1987, 1988

Published by *Macmillan Publishers Ltd*
London and Basingstoke
Associated companies and representatives in Accra,
Auckland, Delhi, Dublin, Gaborone, Hamburg, Harare,
Hong Kong, Kuala Lumpur, Lagos, Manzini, Melbourne,
Mexico City, Nairobi, New York, Singapore, Tokyo

ISBN 0–333–41394–6

Printed in Hong Kong

British Library Cataloguing in Publication Data
Dyde, Brian S.
  Antigua and Barbuda: the heart of the Caribbean.
  1. Antigua and Barbuda — Description and travel —
  Guide-books
  I. Title
  917.297'404   F2035

ISBN 0–333–41394–6

To   *T.G.J. Joseph*
  my tutor in the university of Antigua

Contents

Maps

Maps drawn by the author

Photographic acknowledgements
The author and publishers wish to acknowledge, with thanks, the following photographic sources.

Anne Bolt pp 5; 32; 33; 38; 41; 42; 56; 57; 64; 78; 85; 105; 112; 116; 138; Michael Bourne pp 50; 53; 72; 94; Paddy Browne pp 13; 25; 39; 76; 83; 88; 93; 101; Brian Dyde pp 9; 28; 99; George Earnshaw p 16; R P ffrench pp 20; 21; G W Lennox pp 44; 66; Tony and Jenny Meston pp 4; 122; 126; 127; St James's Club p 103 (both photographs); Tropical Studios pp 131; 139;
Cover photograph: Anne Bolt

The publishers have made every effort to trace the copyright holders, but if they have inadvertently overlooked any, they will be pleased to make the necessary arrangements at the first opportunity.

Acknowledgements

My warmest thanks go to the people who helped in my research for this book. The following provided me with ready access to library books, answered many questions, lent me personal books and documents, and gave much useful advice and information: Edris Bird, Julia Braithwaite, Burt Joseph, T.G. J. Joseph, Sharon Knight, Leslie Lett, Phyllis Mayers, Claire McLean, and the staff of the National Archives.

   I am especially grateful to Peggy Henry for unselfishly giving me access to her 'little red book' of Antiguan proverbs, and for allowing a selection to be printed. My biggest debt of gratitude is to my wife, Veronica, for her patience, encouragement and assistance throughout the writing of the book. Needless to say the opinions expressed and any mistakes made are all my own.

Foreword

Antigua and Barbuda are two small islands about twenty-seven miles apart in the eastern Caribbean. The great majority of Antiguans have never seen let alone visited Barbuda, and it is very likely that a sizeable number of Barbudans have never been to Antigua. The State however is made up of *three* islands – the third being called Redonda, a much smaller island about thirty miles to the south-west of Antigua. Redonda can be seen clearly from Antigua on most days, but is invisible from Barbuda; it is rarely visited by anyone, having been deserted for the past sixty years or so.

I believe this rather unusual state of affairs with regard to the composition of a single country illustrates something of the individuality and independent outlook of the people of both Antigua and Barbuda. At the same time it provides a good example of an irrational State created as a result of decisions reached merely to achieve administrative tidiness in the colonial past. Barbuda was annexed to Antigua in 1860 as a way out of intractable problems concerned with the administration of the former, and to try to stabilise the relationship between the inhabitants of the two islands. Redonda, which is considerably closer to both Montserrat and Nevis than to Antigua, was annexed in 1869 only because Antigua was then the administrative centre for the whole of the Leeward Islands Colony. Had the seat of government for this colony been in, say, St Kitts at this time it is most unlikely that either Barbuda or Redonda would now have any connection with Antigua.

I became aware while carrying out research for this book, and possibly arising from the way the State was formed, that a number of myths and quite false impressions concerning all three islands have entered local folklore, which are repeated and embellished in travel books, newspaper articles and endless tourist literature. Local readers must be prepared to discover that some cherished 'facts' and statistics concerning their country have little basis in truth. Who, after all, ever carried out a survey and counted one beach in Antigua for every day of the year, or found an archaeologist prepared to give credence to the erection of 'megaliths' on Green Castle Hill? My exposure of some of these myths should offend no one; Antigua and Barbuda has more than enough to offer visitors without the need to dress up its appeal with fables and half-truths.

Because of the large disparity in development, resources and population between the two islands, inevitably this book must be primarily a guide to Antigua. Barbuda, which has a unique history and offers fewer but very different attractions from those of Antigua, is the subject of one chapter, together with a brief description of Redonda. While recognising that Barbudans are proud of their island and very conscious of their individuality, if awkward syntax is to be avoided any general comments about Antiguans which follow must be taken to apply equally to citizens of both islands.

Part one

Background

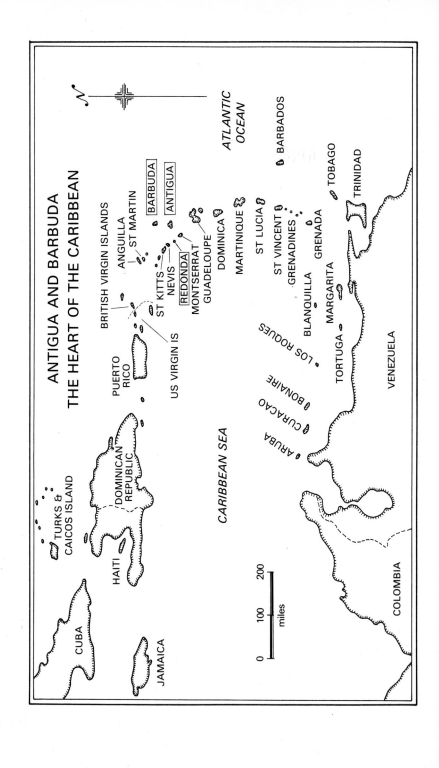

ANTIGUA AND BARBUDA
THE HEART OF THE CARIBBEAN

Chapter one

Introduction

Antigua – 'the heart of the Caribbean'. Can this really be so? If we consider Antigua's place in the huge arc of islands stretching from the southern tip of Florida to the coast of Venezuela, then the answer must be 'no'. But there are many 'Caribbeans': are we talking about the *geographer's* Caribbean, the *political* Caribbean, the *English-speaking* Caribbean, the *tourists'* Caribbean, or what? For most of the population of Antigua the Caribbean consists of those islands between Puerto Rico in the north-west and Trinidad in the south. For the majority of English-speaking visitors, I would suggest that if we exclude Jamaica and the Bahamas the same definition applies.

It is not the purpose of this book to try to prove that Antigua is in fact at the heart or hub of the Caribbean, but to provide a general view of the island and its people from which readers may draw their own conclusions. However it is impossible to write about Antigua without stressing the importance of its location and natural facilities. Nor is it possible to write about the Antiguan people and their recent history without showing that their endeavours and achievements have reached a level far ahead of that found in many other islands in the region. By virtue of her geographical position and the continuing development of her human and natural resources it will be seen, I hope, that Antigua has a just claim to be considered as 'the heart of the Caribbean'.

This assertion is made in many of the tourist brochures, together with claims that Antigua is 'a holiday haven', 'a tourist paradise', and a place 'where land and sea make beauty'. The island does have much to offer the tourist and vacationer – indeed its economy depends on this fact – but there is much more than 'a

A cruise ship leaving Deep Water Harbour, Antigua

'Small Island Girl'

land of perpetual sunshine' peopled by the shadowy adjuncts to the 'perfect vacation' of travel agents and tour operators. For the ordinary Antiguan the real island lies, literally, behind the beaches, the hotels and all the vacation pastimes involving sea, sun, rum punches and steel bands. Other than a multitude of superb beaches, Antigua has a limited number of 'sights' and 'tourist attractions'. The majority could be seen in a couple of days by those who are interested only in places and not in people.

It is the Antiguan people themselves that make Antigua what it is. They are not there as human ornamentation of the 'sights', nor are they waiting to be pitied for the all too obvious signs of poverty here and there in the island. They are a people who have only just become possessors of their own country (the final vestiges of colonial rule disappeared as recently as 1981), and they are now busy trying to create a true nation. The island lives up to all the purple prose of the tourist brochures, but this forms only a facade

– behind which the visitor can find the true and more rewarding Antigua.

Throughout the English-speaking West Indies there is an accepted code of greeting which is widely observed. The basic rule is that the person arriving – the visitor to a house, the customer in a shop, the client entering an office – is the one who makes the opening remark. While in other parts of the world it may be unimportant who greets whom, or who speaks first, this is not so in Antigua. As with a private visitor to a house so it is with a visitor to Antigua. In very general terms you, the visitor, are expected to open any dialogue. The Antiguan is here already, you are entering his country, so common politeness means that you should acknowledge the relationship. Countless visitors have discovered that a 'Good morning', delivered at the right time and with the proper intonation, has opened up a new and far richer view of Antigua and Antiguan society. Antiguans are naturally friendly, polite and helpful, but only towards those who are prepared to show that they are well-disposed and wish to be friendly. Inevitably some visitors will find fault – the poor state of the roads, perhaps, or undue surliness in a petty official. While not in any way seeking to excuse the absence of any of the niceties of life or social behaviour, I feel it may be worthwhile for anyone made conscious of such shortcomings to reflect on one or two aspects of Antiguan history.

In terms of European settlement Antigua is as old as the USA. The first English settlers arrived in the island only twelve years after the *Mayflower* brought the Pilgrim Fathers to New England. After that, while the history of the USA shows constant change combined with the development of its resources and the advancement of its people, the same cannot be said of its tiny neighbour in the Caribbean. Under British colonial rule very little of interest to the outside world – other than the introduction and subsequent abolition of slavery – occurred in Antigua from the first settlement until well into the present century. This is shown only too clearly by the very limited amount written about the history of the island before the outbreak of the Second World War. In 1844 an anonymous author (now known to have been a Mrs Lanaghan, the English wife of a planter) published a two-volume 'full account of the colony and its inhabitants from the time of the Caribs to the present day'. *Antigua and the Antiguans* is an enlightening and very readable book (as will be seen I hope from the extracts quoted hereafter), but only about half of one volume is concerned with the history of the island; the remainder being devoted to observations on its appearance, natural history, and the social life of its inhabitants, both black and white. But even this amount of history is considerably more than that found in another book published in 1894, which claimed to be *The History of the Island of Antigua*. This is a work in three enormous volumes written by Vere Langford Oliver, consisting of nothing more than a colossal list of the pedigrees of the white Antiguan proprietary families, with an insignificant amount of historical detail concerning Antigua.

The modern history of the island can be said to have begun in 1939, when the struggle to end colonial rule started in earnest just as the Second World War broke out. Within two years the circumstances of war brought US servicemen and civilian contractors to Antigua in large numbers. Thereafter, as Antiguans continued along the road to independence from Great Britain, their fortunes became more and more involved with those of North America. The influence of the USA, and later Canada, increased as the dominance of Great Britain in Antiguan affairs slowly waned and eventually disappeared. Today, with the British influence on the social and cultural life remaining as strong as ever, but with the State steadily increasing its economic ties with North America, Antigua is nicely balanced between the Old and New Worlds.

The significance of the major events in Antigua's history having taken place within the past fifty years cannot be over-stressed. Full adult suffrage was granted only in 1951; genuine internal self-government came about in 1967, and complete independence in 1981. Few Antiguans would advance any of these facts as excuses for any inadequacy in sociability or social amenities. Despite this, the visitor with a genuine interest in Antigua and her people can only benefit from keeping them in mind.

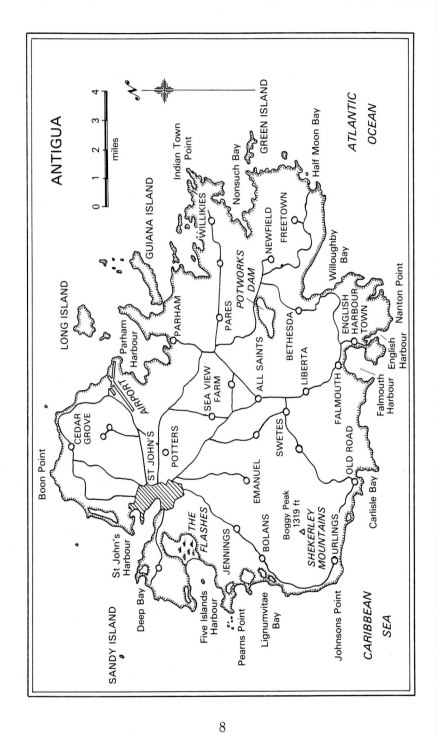

Chapter two

The island

Location and formation

Antigua is in the middle of the Leeward Islands which form the most northerly group of the Lesser Antilles. It is about 450 miles to the east of Hispaniola and the same distance to the north of Trinidad. Unlike most of the islands which form the eastern boundary of the Caribbean Sea it is not of volcanic origin. Instead it is formed of mainly sedimentary rocks, chiefly limestone, with the remains of very ancient volcanic activity in one corner of the island only. It sits on the southern edge of a large bank of relatively shallow water about 1200 square miles in area, with Barbuda at the northern end. With an area of about 108 square miles Antigua

The 'Sleeping Indian' as seen from Marble Hill

is very roughly oval in shape. The coastline is so irregular though, with deep bays and creeks, that to compare the island with any regular shape must stretch the imagination. There are a number of small islets close offshore, together with large areas of reefs and shoals. These reefs have made the approaches from seaward difficult throughout Antigua's history. At the same time they provide excellent protection for many of the bays, and the island has always had a reputation for possessing some of the best harbours in the West Indies.

Antigua can be divided into three main regions. The area to the south and west of a line drawn from Five Islands Harbour on the west coast to Falmouth Harbour on the south coast is the highest part. It consists of steep hills of volcanic formation, several of which are over 1000 feet in height. The highest point in the island called Boggy Peak is only just over 1300 feet high. The hills are covered with green vegetation, and this has given rise to the impression that they contain a tropical rain forest. In fact there are no forests of any kind in Antigua. The area also contains many steep-sided valleys which in wet weather hold fast-flowing streams. This again could give a misleading impression as there are no permanent rivers or streams in this or any other part of the island.

The central part of Antigua is an undulating plain about three miles wide, which runs diagonally across the island from St John's Harbour in the north-west to Willoughby Bay in the south-east. The boundary between this plain and the higher, more hilly country to the north is marked by a very broken limestone escarpment. This is steep in places and can be readily identified to the north of St John's, and more so where it forms the cliff-like north shore of Willoughby Bay.

Climate

The main reason why there are no forests or rivers in Antigua is because the island does not get enough rainfall. It lies directly in the path of the North-East Trade Winds, and the wind blows from the east for ninety per cent of the time. With little high ground and no forests to attract rainfall the annual average figure for the whole island is about 45 inches. As the ground in the central plain is unsuitable for deep penetration of water an enormous proportion of rain-water runs into the sea. Most of what passes into the subsoil is collected in the hilly south-western region. Throughout its history the island has suffered from prolonged droughts and a general shortage of fresh water. The problem has been tackled in a variety of ways. In the past wells were sunk in areas where ground water collected, and numerous small ponds were created for the use of animals and subsistence farmers. Since the first buildings were erected it has been the practice to collect rain-water from the roofs in tanks or cisterns, and still today this provides the main supply of fresh water in the majority of Antiguan houses. In the late 1960s a large, shallow reservoir was constructed in the centre of the island to provide the main source of a piped fresh water supply. Today, with an increasing population and an expanding tourist industry, the total supply of fresh water can barely meet the demand. In 1985 it was decided to deal with this problem by constructing a desalination plant on the north coast. When completed this should produce enough extra fresh water to meet the demand for many years to come.

The low rainfall and more or less constant easterly breeze gives Antigua one of the finest climates in the West Indies. There are no wet and dry seasons as such. Based on records compiled during the past 120 years the most that can be said is that – in an average year – September, October and November are *likely* to be the rainiest months, and February, March and April the driest. The warmest time of the year is between August and October, when the temperature range is from 80-89°F. The coolest months are December, January and February, with a temperature range of about 70-80°F. These idyllic conditions are interrupted from time to time by the passage of a hurricane or a tropical storm – to which the whole of the Caribbean region is prone in certain months. The 'hurricane season' lasts from the middle of July to the middle of October, with August being the month in which they are most likely to occur. The well-known old rhyme sums it up:

> *June, too soon;*
> *July, stand by;*
> *August, come it must.*
> *September, remember;*
> *October, all over.*

11

Antigua has not experienced one since 1950, and those that have passed in the vicinity since then have only produced much-needed heavy rain.

Earthquakes

It would be inappropriate not to mention that Antigua, besides being threatened by the possibility of a hurricane each year, is also subject to occasional earth tremors and very infrequent earthquakes. The majority of the tremors are so minor as to pass quite unnoticed. The most recent earthquake was in 1974 when a few public buildings, particularly in St John's, were damaged. The threat from such earth movements is by no means as great as in places like San Francisco or Tokyo, and with no densely populated areas or high-rise buildings the danger to life is minimal.

The coastline

No description of Antigua would be complete without mention of three features of the coastline – the beaches, the salt ponds and the reefs. Popular local opinion holds that the island has 365 beaches; one for each day of the year. While this may or may not be so (and there is certainly no documentary evidence of their existence) Antigua has an extremely long coastline for such a small island. This is over 90 miles in length and there are ample bays and coves containing stretches of fine white sand. These beaches form one of Antigua's greatest natural attractions, and some of them rank amongst the finest in the entire Caribbean.

The salt ponds which are found behind many of the beaches, especially along the west coast, are another distinctive feature. They were probably created by shallow bays being cut off from the sea by the growth of mangroves and other plants. These caused sand to be deposited and to build up into bars, and allowed the enclosed water to become brackish. Eventually they turned into the swamps or shallow ponds that are seen today. The largest single area, called The Flashes, is at the head of Five Islands Harbour. In recent years attempts have been made to create

A stretch of Antigua's more rugged coastline

artificial boat harbours in one or two of the smaller ponds, by
dredging through the sand bar separating them from the sea. None
has been successful as the natural action of the sea which created
the bars has proved too intractable. The ponds are of considerable
ecological importance, and some which contain evidence of the
pre-historic habitation of the island have great archaeological
interest. Current thinking from the conservation point of view is
that it would be unwise to tamper with any of them.

The extensive areas of coral reef, particularly on the northern
and eastern sides of the island, are another prime national asset. A
more or less continuous barrier reef about two miles offshore,
containing areas with names such as Salt Fish Tail, Horseshoe
Reef and Kettle Bottom Shoals, protects the whole of the north
coast. From Long Island around the north-east coast as far as
Green Island there are an enormous number of coral reefs and

patches surrounding each islet, and extending across the mouth of each bay and inlet. In the south-east Willoughby Bay is cut off at its entrance by a much bigger Horseshoe Reef, through which there are narrow passages, while the whole of the shoreline between Falmouth Harbour and the south-western corner of the island is fringed by coral. About a mile offshore to the south of Johnsons Point in the south-west is Cades Reef – a huge area of reef about one and a half square miles in extent and within a few feet of the surface. While all of these reefs are of course highly dangerous to shipping they are a most important natural resource. Besides assisting in the creation of the island's splendid beaches, they also provide a breeding and feeding ground for many varieties of fish and shellfish. They also protect the windward coasts from erosion and provide calm water in the bays and inshore passages.

Chapter three

Natural history

Plants

On the first approach the coast appears rough and barren, but as the voyager draws nearer, hills and valleys open on his view, and the shore puts on an appearance of luxuriant vegetation.

While this description from the opening pages of *Antigua and the Antiguans* still holds true today, the appearance of the island from a distance is as deceptive now as it was in the 1840s. The forest with which the island was covered when it was sighted by Columbus in 1493 disappeared long before Mrs Lanaghan's day, and the luxuriant aspect is created by large areas of bush interspersed with farmland. The hilly region contains plenty of trees with mahogany, logwood and cedar growing together with coconut and other palms, mango and breadfruit trees, to give the closest approximation to a forest in Antigua. The rest of the island is very open, with large tracts of pasture, arable land and bush well intermingled, and with the occasional grove of trees or small coconut plantations. Most of the bush consists of various species of acacia, all of which are referred to locally as 'cassie'.

Around the coast, providing shade at the back of most beaches, are coconut, tamarind and casuarina, together with sea-grape and manchineel trees. The sea-grape is a low tree with large broad leaves which bears clusters of small velvety berries which, when ripe and purple in colour, are edible. The notorious manchineel on the other hand is to be avoided; the sap is caustic and poisonous as are the small apple-like fruit. Mangrove trees grow profusely around the heads of some of the bays and creeks, especially on

15

Bougainvillaea makes a splash of colour at the Blue Waters Hotel

16

the north-east coast between Parham Harbour and Mercers Creek Bay.

As if to offset the vast expanse of green vegetation, whether wild or cultivated, which covers most of the island, Antiguans grow a profusion of flowering trees and shrubs. At any time of the year many varieties of hibiscus, oleander and bougainvillaea, usually grown as hedges, will be seen in the garden of even the smallest house. The flamboyant or poinciana tree, which bears a bright red flower, is also very common.

In the same small garden with its hibiscus or oleander hedge almost always there will be at least one kind of fruit tree. Although little fruit, other than pineapples, is grown on a proper commercial basis, there are few householders who do not have a lime, breadfruit, mango, paw-paw, guava or some other fruit tree 'in the yard'. Some fruit are picked all the year round while others have their seasons, but there is always a big selection available. The surplus from the larger private orchards and the produce of small market gardens inevitably finds a retail outlet, and all the fruit mentioned above and many more can be found on sale around the island.

The innate conservatism of the standard hotel menu prevents many varieties of local fruit from appearing on it. The visitor who accepts this and foregoes the opportunity of sampling a grafted mango, a paw-paw or a sugar apple, bought from a street huckster, will miss a rare treat. The visitor who finds such things on the menu will know that he is staying in a superior hotel. (Having said this, a word of advice concerning one of these fruit may be necessary. The proper way to eat a mango is to attack it with one's teeth, ignoring any attempt at delicacy with knife, fork or spoon. A ripe, grafted juli mango eaten while standing or sitting in the sea is unbelievably good – the salt water adding to the flavour and washing away all traces of the flesh and juice which, if the mango is to be enjoyed to the full, must gather on the eater's face . . .)

Animals

The wild animal life of Antigua is very limited. Indeed, as Mrs Lanaghan pointed out, 'In an island like Antigua, destitute of every wild animal of larger growth than a rabbit or a rat, it may be deemed risible to talk about its zoology ...' Today it is highly unlikely that there are any rabbits remaining on the island as the 'rat' to which she referred was probably the mongoose, which had been introduced during the 18th century. This animal was brought to the West Indies to keep down the rats and snakes in the sugar cane fields. In Antigua it soon rid the island of all its snakes, but when it began to attack poultry and the wild bird life it was realised that its introduction was not an unqualified blessing. Throughout the West Indies the mongoose is now classified as a pest: in Antigua it is probably the only wild animal that most visitors will ever see.

Although there are no snakes left there are numerous lizards. The common tree lizard will be seen on almost any tree or fence. Normally green it has the power of changing its colour like a chameleon. It feeds on insects and small buds and is perfectly harmless. The ground lizard, which is much larger and darker, will sometimes be seen, or more likely heard, scuttling about among fallen leaves and vegetation. It too is harmless and will run away if approached. Anyone who sights an even bigger member of the lizard family, the iguana, will be very fortunate. These are found only in the drier eastern part of the island, well away from all human habitation, and sightings in recent years have been very rare.

Birds

The bird life of Antigua is considerably more interesting than the animal life, but is still not prolific. The bird population appears to fluctuate from year to year, being very sensitive to the amount of rainfall and the effect this has on the number of insects available for food. Over 140 species have been observed, of which about 90 are seen regularly. The ornithologist will find much of interest at any time of the year as many of the species are migratory and the bird population varies from season to season. Some of the more common resident birds are so much in evidence that they cannot fail to be noticed by even the most casual observer.

Just as the banana is probably the most common fruit in Antigua, a small, yellow-breasted bird called the Bananaquit is one of the commonest birds. This can be seen any day together with another bird of much the same size, the Lesser Antillean Bullfinch, which is black or grey with a reddish breast. These are seen around most hotels with outdoor dining areas, and they are fond of taking sugar and crumbs from the tables. One or two species of humming bird are native to the island, and these will be seen and heard around any flowering shrub. The commonest is probably the Antillean Crested Hummingbird, which is very small and dark with a bright green crest. In the countryside the most conspicuous bird is the Cattle Egret, a small white heron with a bright yellow bill. It is seen in the company of grazing animals, often standing on the back of a cow, or where ploughing is taking place. In the evenings large roosts of these birds are found in the trees around various ponds.

Anywhere around the coast the Brown Pelicans are unmistakable. They are usually sighted in small groups either sitting on rocks or flying low over the sea. They are spectacular birds in flight and make a lot of noise when diving into the water after fish. That this bird is very common can be discovered from a quick glance at a map of Antigua, on which are shown no less than three Pelican Islands and a group of Pelican Rocks. Many other varieties of shore birds and waders frequent the salt ponds and reservoirs. Several species of gulls and terns live on some of the small islets off the north-east coast, where Great Bird Island, Little Bird Island, Bird Island and Bird Islet presumably all take their names from the birds' habitats.

A Guide to the Birds of Antigua by William Spencer is a booklet compiled by a local resident which gives details of some of the commoner birds and their habitats. Copies are readily available from a number of shops in St John's. For more detailed information it will be necessary to refer to *Birds of the West Indies*, the standard work by James Bond.

The Bananaquit

Marine life

The waters around Antigua abound with marine life, but contain little that need bother the swimmer, snorkeler or skin-diver. As in any tropical waters there are potentially troublesome things such as sharks, barracuda, spiney sea urchins and, at certain times of the year, large jellyfish. There have been very few reports of sharks coming close inshore within living memory, and the observation of elementary precautions will ensure that none of the others need worry anyone in the sea. The diver or swimmer experienced enough to venture out to the more distant reefs will presumably

20

The Brown Pelican

know and observe the basic rules about not poking into crevices, bleeding in the water or making a lot of noise. The less adventurous will find the shallow water off a beach virtually devoid of marine life, but it is unwise to wade where the seabed is covered by seaweed (the most common type is called eelgrass) as this may hide sea urchins.

Apart from the great variety of coral formations and their attendant tropical fish to be seen by the snorkeler and diver, the sea around Antigua also supports many types of edible fish. The local fishermen are able to provide a reasonable supply of fish such as Grouper, Parrotfish, Snapper and Grunts, as well as lobsters, to meet the local demand. There are also fish such as Kingfish, Marlin, Wahoo and Tuna to interest the sport fishing enthusiast. Most species migrate annually through the eastern Caribbean chain of islands, and the best season for Antigua is from February to June.

Chapter four

A brief history

Pre-Columbus

There is evidence that the island we now know as Antigua has been inhabited, although not continuously, for about the past 4000 years. The earliest known inhabitants were the Siboney ('Stone people'), of whom not much is recorded except that they were nomadic and had no knowledge of agriculture. Some stone tools and evidence of their considerable consumption of shellfish have been discovered at one or two places around the coast. The first people to leave behind any major evidence of their occupation of the island were the Arawaks. These probably reached Antigua about two thousand years ago. They originated in South America and gradually spread through the island chain of the eastern Caribbean. They practised agriculture and developed a settled village life. Lots of tools, pottery fragments and decorated shells have been unearthed at several sites, again on or near the coast.

The Arawak occupation probably ended in about 1200AD when they moved on to other islands further west, or were overrun by the Caribs. These people, who of course have given their name to the Caribbean Sea, also originated in South America and spread northwards through the islands. They were much more war-like and less pastoral than the Arawaks. No trace has yet been found of their settlement of the island, but they continued to visit it – often with bloody results – until the end of the 17th century. Based on rather slender evidence (an unverified entry in a Carib-French dictionary of the mid-17th century) it is thought that the Carib name for the island was something like 'Waladli' – a disagreeably unmelodious appellation very much in keeping with the nature of their society. Their name for Barbuda, from the same source, was even more unpleasant. The reader has only to ask herself if she would like a vacation in, or enjoy being a citizen of, the 'State of Waladli and Wa'omoni' to appreciate the debt owed by at least two West Indian islands to the first European discoverer.

Discovery and settlement

In November 1493, on his second voyage to the New World, Columbus sighted the island and gave it the name *Santa Maria la Antigua* (after a famous statue of The Virgin in Seville Cathedral). In doing so he not only started its recorded history but provided it with a name of considerable grace and harmony, even though it was soon shortened to just Antigua. And here perhaps is the place to stress that the name is pronounced as 'Anteega' and not as if it rhymed with 'how big you are'. Columbus did not land and very little happened in the island for the next 130 years. The Spanish, English and French made desultory efforts at settlement, but failed through the lack of fresh water and raids by the Caribs. The first permanent European settlement was founded in 1632, when a group of English colonists arrived from the nearby island of St Kitts which had been settled some eight years earlier. The first settlement was in the south in the area now called Old Road. Except for a few months in 1666 and 1667 when the French occupied it, Antigua remained in British hands thereafter.

Plantations and slavery

To begin with the island was used for growing tobacco (another word from the Carib language), but by the end of the 17th century this had been replaced totally by sugar cane. The production of sugar was far more profitable and it remained the basis of the economy until well into the second half of the 20th century. For the first thirty years or so after the initial settlement the population was very small. It began to rise quickly only when the conversion from tobacco to sugar production started. The planters found that indentured white servants and labourers gave poor results, and so turned to the importation of slaves from Africa to work their plantations. In 1680 the population was about 4500, made up of almost equal numbers of whites and blacks. Thirty years later the white population had increased only fractionally while the black proportion had swelled to nearly 13 000. As Antigua progressed through the 18th century the planters became firmly established as men of wealth and substance. With an economy based entirely on sugar being produced by an army of slaves, the island was divided up into numerous estates (a map of the early 19th century lists 161 by name). Each estate was centred

Ffryes Mill

on an 'estate house' and had at least one windmill to grind the cane and extract the juice.

The estate system has had an ineradicable effect on the island. Most of the estate names remain in use, serving as district names outside the villages and within the six parishes into which, outside St John's, Antigua is divided. The windmills, now of course all abandoned and sail-less, can be seen everywhere. They are an enduring and in some ways most befitting memorial to the succeeding generations of slaves who operated them. The estate houses, which a writer in the early 1800s described as being '... embosomed in trees having more of the appearance of country mansions in England than almost any others in the West Indies' have largely disappeared or fallen into disrepair. Those which are still inhabited or have been converted to some other use excite very little interest. The stone towers of the windmills on the other hand remain conspicuous and intriguing in every part of the island: impervious to weather, hurricanes and earthquakes they are seemingly indestructible.

Emancipation and the decline of sugar

Sugar production continued to be extremely profitable until towards the end of the 18th century. After that, as Great Britain found other cheaper sources of sugar, the economy of Antigua began to decline. This decline matched the increase in the demands for an end to slavery. The slave trade was made illegal by Great Britain in 1807, and this was followed in 1834 by the abolition of slavery itself. In Antigua at that time there were just over 29 000 slaves, about 4000 'Free Coloureds' and barely 2000 whites.

The slaves were made completely free on 1 August 1834, but within a few weeks of their emancipation the majority had returned to the estates to work as free labourers. They had little choice as there were very few areas of free land available for them to settle on and cultivate. Those that refused to continue living on an estate began to settle in 'independent villages' with names like Freetown, Liberta and Freemans Village. Others went to live in villages which grew up around Non-conformist churches which

26

had ministered to them while they were still slaves – places like Newfield, Bethesda and All Saints. By 1842 nearly thirty villages had been established and the map of Antigua began to take on the aspect it bears today.

As the freed slaves and their descendants started along the road to full political independence, the economy continued to wane. This was brought about by the fall in the value of West Indian sugar and by the unwillingness of the planters to turn to other crops. As a result many estates were either abandoned or incorporated into others as the 19th century progressed. By the beginning of the present century ownership of the estates was in the hands of comparatively few proprietors. By the mid-1940s most of the arable land belonged to one company. The effect this had on the ordinary Antiguan, the quality of his life and his standard of living, was devastating. A field worker's daily rate of pay in 1845 was one shilling; one hundred years later it varied between one and one and a half shillings if he worked on a large estate, and was *less* than one shilling if he had the misfortune to be employed on a small estate. Throughout this period Antigua remained a British colony, with a Governor exercising power through his Executive and Legislative Councils. Half of the members only of the latter were elected, with the electorate confined to whites and those blacks who could meet certain property and income qualifications.

The rise of Trade Unionism and the Second World War

The first major event to upset this depressing and stagnant state of affairs took place in 1939 with the passing of the Trade Union Act. This permitted the workers to act together to press for higher wages, better conditions and shorter hours. The first Trade Union in Antigua was registered the following year. Although this had an immediate effect on the life of the island a much greater event – the outbreak of the Second World War – must be considered as even more important to the creation of the Antigua we see today.

In an agreement with Great Britain reached in 1941 the USA leased sites for military bases in Antigua and other West Indian islands. In Antigua the arrival of large numbers of American servicemen and civilian contractors, and the need to erect their

Deep Water Harbour, St John's

base facilities in a hurry, had an immediate and lasting effect on the way of life. To begin with local labour was hired at wage rates much higher than those paid by local employers. The 1941 sugar crop suffered from a shortage of field labourers, and many men refused to return to that kind of work from then on. As the war progressed the bases also provided some technical training. Labourers who remained working on them had the opportunity to become skilled or semi-skilled technicians – something most would have considered inconceivable in 1939.

While it would not be true to say that the presence of so many Americans in the island (the population of which at the time was about 40 000) did not have its unpleasant aspects, the overall effect was to the benefit of the Antiguan people. The island gained materially from the construction of roads, deep water piers, and most of all a proper air field. The bases themselves were run down quickly after the war ended, but by then it must have been obvious that the Caribbean region would remain very much within the sphere of influence of the USA. By 1945 many ordinary Antiguans had been given a glimpse of another way of life and the opportunities it had to offer. There remained the problems of bringing these opportunities within their grasp, and of ending the dependence of the island's economy on sugar. It was to solving these problems that the Antigua Trades and Labour Union started to devote its energies as soon as the war was over. By that time the Union had a new President, elected in 1943. In Vere Cornwall Bird the Antiguan people were to find a man with the energy, intelligence and political ability to deal with the problems, and to lead them along the final stretch of the hard and sometimes very bumpy road to independent nationhood.

V.C. Bird and independence

In 1945 Bird was elected to the Legislative Council, and he began his connection with the government of Antigua which has continued for over forty years. Mostly through his efforts and those of a few of his colleagues in the Antigua Labour Party full adult suffrage was granted in 1951, followed five years later by the introduction of a Ministerial system of Government. The Executive Council with its nominated members remained, but now contained three full-time Ministers, of whom Bird was one. In 1961 further constitutional changes were introduced. The number of elected members to the Legislative Council was increased and Bird became the Chief Minister with responsibility for choosing his own Ministers from among the Council members. In 1965, having demonstrated that black Antiguans were quite capable of running their own country, Bird and his Government began negotiations with the British Government about ending colonial rule. These led to Antigua being granted independence 'in association with Great Britain' in February 1967. Under this new relationship Antigua had full control over its internal affairs, but left the responsibility for defence and external affairs in British hands. Bird of course became the island's first Premier.

Throughout the years leading up to 'Associated Statehood' the role of sugar as the dominant factor in the economy had declined steadily. By 1965 Antigua Syndicate Estates, the company which by then owned all the sugar estates and the single sugar factory, was in great financial trouble. Two years later, in order to protect the jobs of several thousand workers and to secure the land for the people of Antigua, the assets of the company were bought by the Government. It was somehow very befitting that the last vestiges of the 'Plantocracy' should have disappeared in the same year that Antigua achieved Statehood. Bird was out of office between 1971 and 1976, and it was during this period that the sugar crop was abandoned and the factory closed down. In 1972, some 300 years after the crop was introduced, the reign of 'King Sugar' in Antigua came to an end.

The island remained an Associated State until 1 November 1981, when it became the major part of the totally independent country of Antigua and Barbuda. By then Bird had dominated the political scene for so long that all Antiguans, regardless of their colour, background or political affiliations, must have felt it only right and proper that he should become the State's first Prime Minister. It is worth repeating that the majority of the important events in Antiguan history have taken place since 1939. This is well within the lifetime of a considerable proportion of the present population. During that period British Governors and Administrators came and went – few leaving any lasting impression on the island – while Bird has been there throughout, his name synonymous with Antigua. He remains there today, the unchallenged leader of his country, dominating life and politics just as the old windmill towers continue to dominate the remains of the estates they once served.

Chapter five

The economy

Agriculture

Until after the Second World War the economy of Antigua depended almost entirely on the production of sugar cane. Sugar, molasses and rum accounted for well over ninety per cent of the island's exports up until 1945. After the war the agricultural scene began to change. The independent small farmers were encouraged to grow Sea Island Cotton, for which parts of the island are very well suited, and crops such as arrowroot and castor. The limiting factor to any agricultural diversification though was the unpredictable rainfall and the absence of streams or ponds for irrigation. A great deal to improve the situation had been carried out by the mid-1960s with the construction of earth-filled dams to form small reservoirs and ponds. By then sugar had become a marginal crop (disappearing altogether in 1972) and agricultural activity was concentrated on the growing of cotton, fruit and vegetables, and in the rearing of livestock.

Except that attempts are being made to revive the sugar industry on a small scale in order to meet purely local requirements, the agricultural scene remains much the same today. The cotton crop has a guaranteed market in the Far East and is slowly being increased. Fruit and vegetables are grown almost exclusively for local consumption, although a good overseas market exists for the famous Antigua 'Black' pineapple. Cattle, sheep, goats and pigs are also reared for a purely local market. It will be obvious to even the most casual visitor that much of the island is uncultivated, and that large areas of what could be useful agricultural land are covered in bush and scrub.

31

Picking cotton

Probably less than five per cent of the total work-force is engaged in agriculture.

From being the basis of the island's economy for well over three hundred years, agriculture has become the least important factor in the space of perhaps one generation. Considering the long history of the estate system it is easy to understand why working on the land should be despised and rejected by so many Antiguans, but it is no less unfortunate that this should be the attitude. If the overall development of the State is to continue it will be important to utilise the land – one of its chief assets – to the full. The present official programme of encouraging the introduction of new crops and farming methods, while stimulating agricultural research and the involvement of foreign investors, is slowly changing the prevailing attitude. It is inconceivable that large numbers of Antiguans will ever be attracted back to the land, but there is no reason why, in time and with the proper assistance, the island's agricultural potential should not be realised.

The beach of the Blue Waters Hotel, on the north coast

Industry

Before about 1970 anyone talking about a factory in Antigua could only have been referring to the *sugar* factory. The manufacturing industry at that time comprised a rum distillery, a cotton ginnery, an edible oil plant, a few small furniture workshops, the odd pottery and one or two boat yards producing wooden boats. In 1965 the construction of a large (for the size of the island) oil refinery was begun on land to the north of St John's, which started operations two years later. The concept that this was something around which the industrial development of the island could be built was quickly destroyed by the oil fuel crisis of 1973-74. The refinery was forced to close down less than ten years after it opened. An attempt to reactivate it in the early 1980s proved abortive and it is now defunct.

Although the need for an industrial sector in the economy was recognised much earlier, the right conditions for its growth did not come into being until about 1970. By that time deep water port facilities had been constructed on the north side of St John's Harbour, and the airport had been improved and modernised in order to operate all types and sizes of aircraft. Despite the set-back caused by the closure of the oil refinery, the industrialisation of Antigua, in as far as this term can be applied to the island, continued throughout the next decade. The incentives being offered for the setting up of 'pioneer' industries were improved considerably in 1975 by the Fiscal Incentives Act. This made provision for tax holidays, import duty exemptions and the unrestricted repatriation of profits for foreign investors. These incentives, together with the building of a 'factory estate' close to the airport and the presence of a large work-force (with up to twenty per cent unemployment) have had the desired results. Industry, which is fairly evenly divided between local and overseas ownership, is concerned mainly with light manufacturing or assembling enterprises. The goods produced are mostly for the local and regional markets, with one or two for export to North America.

At the same time the number of cottage industries has also increased. Small workshops still make hand-crafted furniture, the traditional wooden boats and ceramic ware. They have now been

34

joined by others, often located in the most unexpected places, producing such things as floor tiles, batteries and concrete garden furniture. The independent spirit of the Antiguan continues to flourish, perhaps in reaction to the advent of the factory and assembly line, but possibly also to the more servile aspects of tourism.

Tourism

The arrival of the US forces in 1941 may have given a few of the more astute Antiguans a foretaste of what lay ahead once the war was over, but it is unlikely that anyone could have foreseen how tourism would come to dominate the economy within the next quarter of a century. In 1950 there was one beach hotel, by 1960 there were seven, and by 1970 the total was nineteen. With the opening of the deep water harbour in 1968 the island started to attract far more cruise ships, and within three years four or five ships were handled each week during the 'tourist season'. After the improvements to the airport carried out in 1970 Antigua was in a position to attract tourists of every sort, not only from North America but from Europe as well. The next decade saw a boom in the construction of guest-houses, apartment and condominium developments, and more hotels.

The tourist industry is now the mainstay of the country's economy and its principal foreign exchange earner. Over 150 000 visitors arrive by air each year, and another 125 000 or so pay shorter visits in the cruise ships. Tourists are offered a complete range of accommodation in nearly forty hotels and numerous guest-houses or apartment complexes of one sort or another. About one sixth of the total work-force is employed directly or indirectly in the industry. The concept of previous years, in which the bulk of visitors came in the fairly short 'season' from mid-December to mid-April, no longer applies. While the numbers fall during the summer months there is plenty of tourist activity throughout the year. Although some of the hotels still close during what used to be called the 'off-season', the visitor is assured of the same service and facilities from the industry as a whole, regardless of the time of year.

The hidden factor

There is one other aspect of the economy, but one about which there is very little information available. This is the contribution made by Antiguans living abroad in the form of cash remittances made to their relatives in the island. It is impossible to measure the overall effect this has on the economy as a whole: at the same time, for anyone acquainted with a cross-section of society, it is impossible not to recognise the importance of this 'hidden factor' to the personal economies of many of the poorer Antiguans.

Chapter six

The people

Population

Antigua, like many of the other small West Indian islands, has a large proportion of its citizens living abroad permanently. Emigration has been a constant factor in the life of the island since at least the beginning of this century. The building of the Panama Canal between 1903 and 1914 attracted many men from Antigua and all the other British West Indian islands. Others emigrated to Cuba, the Dominican Republic, Canada and the USA. The development of oil refineries in the Dutch islands of Curaçao and Aruba in the late 1930s caused more Antiguans to leave, but the largest migration of all took place after the Second World War. This was brought about by the demand for labour in Great Britain, and only halted by the introduction of controls on immigration by the British Government in 1962. Since then Canada and the USA have received the majority of Antiguan emigrants, but limited by the enforcement of quotas and other restrictions.

It is now impossible even to guess at the number of Antiguans living overseas, but it should not be forgotten that they still make a significant contribution to the economy. Those Antiguans who form the island's population number perhaps 80 000 (the last census took place in 1970). The great majority are of African descent, with about ten per cent of mixed black and white ancestry. In none of the censuses taken since 1860 has there ever been more than five per cent of non-African descent, and usually the figure was much smaller; today it is probably less than one per cent, made up of people of British, Portuguese, Syrian and

A happy Antiguan

Lebanese origin. In addition there are possibly two or three
hundred Europeans and North Americans who have retired to
Antigua, or who live in the island for so many months of the year.

These figures only hint at the true composition of Antiguan
society. Before 1962 there were no restrictions on movement
between any of the British West Indian islands. Because of its focal
position in the eastern Caribbean Antigua probably saw more
movement of people, both in and out, than many of the other
islands. As a result many Antiguans were born in other places as
far apart as Guyana and Jamaica, and many more have a parent or
parents born outside the island. It would be stretching the point to
claim that Antiguan society is a Caribbean federation in
microcosm but the diverse origins of the people, black and white,
have helped to create the outward-looking and cosmopolitan
attitude which is now assisting the country's development. The
influence of Great Britain, North America and the rest of the
Caribbean can be traced through many aspects of Antiguan life,
but they are perhaps most apparent in the educational system and
in religious matters.

Education

The State provides free primary and secondary education. There are a few private, fee-paying schools, in some cases affiliated to churches. All provide an education which is grounded very much in the British system and, until recently, orientated towards obtaining British educational certificates and qualifications. The emphasis has now moved towards the use of new curricula developed within the Caribbean region, and a type of education more suited to the social and economic development of the island. The Antigua State College, besides training teachers, also offers technical and vocational training to suit local requirements. Any higher education has to be obtained abroad. Almost invariably this will be at the University of the West Indies (with campuses in Jamaica, Trinidad and Barbados) or at one of the cheaper colleges in the US Virgin Islands, the USA or Canada.

St Peter's Church at Parham

Religion

It must be a matter for some regret that the attempts to create a nation and a sense of nationhood are now, to some extent, being undermined by an unusual degree of divisiveness in religious matters. Even the most transient visitor cannot fail to notice the large number of churches in Antigua. The more innocent might assume that Antiguans are an unusually religious and God-fearing people. Unfortunately this is not quite true, and they are no more and no less devout than any others.

The Christian religion arrived in Antigua with the first settlers, and the Anglican Church remained the 'Established' Church until 1875. In its earlier days, as a local writer the Reverend Leslie Lett has stated, it was '. . . ecclesiastically and racially, entirely and unrepentantly narrow and intolerant . . .' This attitude changed after Emancipation, but long before then the Moravian and Methodist Churches had begun to minister to the slaves and to educate them. As a result the Anglican Church was very much identified with the 'plantocracy' while the mass of the slaves, later the black free labourers, belonged to the Nonconformist Churches. It was a long time before this division ended. Between 1835 and 1882 over 2000 Portuguese came to the island, mostly from Madeira, to work as labourers. While not all of them stayed their continuing presence brought about the establishment of the Roman Catholic Church in Antigua in 1859.

Thereafter, until the 1960s, the Anglican, Moravian, Methodist and Roman Catholic Churches ministered to at least 85 per cent of the population. Since then this proportion has fallen steadily, and in recent years dramatically, with the arrival of numerous fundamentalist Sects and Churches. On the one hand this trend away from the ecumenical leanings of the Churches which originated in Europe and are deeply rooted in the life and history of Antigua, towards the intolerance and occasional bigotry of Churches originating in the southern USA and quite unfamiliar with West Indian life, is to be deplored. On the other hand it can also be viewed as another manifestation of the Antiguan spirit of independence. While every Antiguan has not yet built his own church it often seems, from the ever-increasing number of tabernacles, bethels, halls and temples all around the island, that this must be a common aspiration.

Sport

There is one aspect of life in Antigua which so far has felt little North American influence. The sports played remain very much as in the days when the island was under British rule, and cricket – that most English of games – must be considered the national sport. Indeed, since the inclusion during the 1970s of two Antiguan players in the combined West Indies team which plays at the international level, it has become almost impossible to write about Antigua without mentioning the game. Before Vivian Richards and Anderson Roberts were selected for this team, players from any of the smaller islands had been effectively debarred from playing for the West Indies. Since their selection Antigua has never been quite the same. Both men are folk-heroes who have featured in calypsoes, on postage stamps and at civic receptions. In 1985 Richards was chosen as the captain of the West Indies team. When it is recalled that before 1960 it was inconceivable that a black West Indian, let alone one from a 'small island', could captain the side, it is possible to understand something of the joy with which this news was received in Antigua.

Beach cricket is often played in the evenings after work. No wonder West Indians play so well.

The only other game worth mentioning here is one which should properly be relegated to the status of an indoor table game. Most visitors however will probably see *Warri* – a type of board game for two players – being played outdoors with a degree of noise and movement more suited to more physical and energetic pastimes. The game originates from Africa, as one of the 'hole and pebble' games which started in Egypt over 5000 years ago. The word 'warri' is an African word for houses, and the game is played on a wooden board with two rows of hollows called 'houses', in and out of which each player moves some of his two dozen pebbles ('seeds'). It can be played at a fairly casual level or more seriously using a strategy which matches chess in its range. The game is played in other Caribbean islands but appears to have a much greater following in Antigua, and is now very much identified with the island. Because more has been written about cricket than any

Taxi drivers playing Warri

other game it is impossible to suggest any one book which would explain the game to the uninitiated. But as far as I or the author know there is only one book devoted to explaining the game of Warri. This is *How to play Warri* written by an American, David Chamberlin, but published and printed in Antigua. This deals with both the simple and advanced mechanics of play, and is readily available from shops in St John's.

Government

After independence Antigua and Barbuda remained a monarchy with Queen Elizabeth II as the Head of State. Her representative in the State is the Governor-General. Parliament consists of the House of Representatives and the Senate. Representatives are elected by popular vote from sixteen constituencies in Antigua and one in Barbuda, and a general election must be called at least every five years. Senators are appointed by the Governor-General on the advice of the Prime Minister and the Leader of the Opposition. The Prime Minister heads a Cabinet of Ministers who administer the State. All legislation is introduced in the House of Representatives and then passed to the Senate for review and assent. The whole form of Government is modelled very much on the British Parliamentary System.

While pomp and pageantry play their part in Antigua as much as in Great Britain or elsewhere, there is a degree of informality among the dignitaries and leaders of the States which is very much in keeping with the West Indian way of life. It is not unusual to see the Governor-General at the wheel of his own car, nor to queue with his wife in a local supermarket. Cabinet Ministers and Senators are not the lofty and guarded figures found in some other countries. Ministerial office does not prevent its holder from being stopped for a chat in the street, and most Senators can be found, when the Senate is not sitting, carrying on with perfectly ordinary jobs in St John's.

One important feature of any ceremonial display is of course the national flag. This was flown for the first time when Antigua became an 'Associated State' in 1967. Its various components were

The Antiguan flag

described by the local artist who designed it:

> The red, blue and black to symbolize the dynamism, hope and the African heritage of the Antiguan people; the golden sun to symbolize the dawn of a new era; the gold, blue and white to represent the island's natural attractions of sun, sea and sand; and the 'V' sign to depict victory.

Whether this amount of symbolism should be read into the flag of one tiny nation is open to question, but it certainly cannot be mistaken for the flag of any other country. The design is bold and distinctive, and contrasts beautifully with the normal background of green hills and blue sky. It is flown with pride from public buildings and appears in various representations in most of the tourist literature and on souvenirs of all kinds.

The Courts and the Law

As is to be expected in a Parliamentary democracy, the judiciary is totally independent of the Administration and exercises its authority in accordance with the Constitution and the Laws of Antigua. The regional, as opposed to the purely national, thread can be traced to the High Court judges, who are shared with five other States. Any appointment or dismissal requires the approval of all six States. High Court sentences are subject to review by the Eastern Caribbean Court of Appeal, which sits in Antigua from time to time. Final appeal to the Privy Council in England is still available in some cases. The less serious offences are dealt with in Magistrates' Courts.

Law and order are maintained by the Royal Antigua Police Force, made up of uniformed men and women who do not, in the normal course of events, carry firearms. Once again the regional influence is felt as many members come from other islands, and add to the impartiality of policing a small community. The Police Force is also responsible for the seaward defence of the State. Several small patrol craft are manned which are also used for search and rescue operations when required.

Antigua and the outside world

It is in Antigua's membership of various international and regional organisations that the State acknowledges the three main influences on its life and history. Although it is a member of the British Commonwealth, owing allegiance to a European Queen, Antigua also recognises that it is an integral part of the Caribbean region as well as being very much part of the Americas. Membership of the Organisation of American States was obtained shortly after independence in 1981. Before that Antigua had played an important part in the creation of the Caribbean Community and Common Market (CARICOM), which exists to promote free trade among its members and to protect the growth of local industries. An equally important part was played in establishing the Organisation of Eastern Caribbean States (OECS), in order to extend economic co-operation and to harmonise foreign policy among the seven ex-British Windward and Leeward Islands.

With her membership of both the British Commonwealth and the Organisation of American States Antigua could be said to have a foot in both camps, and to be maintaining links with both the past and the future. With its geographical advantages and present state of development the island is certainly well placed to play a significant role in the future – as the heart of the Caribbean.

Part two

Foreground

Chapter seven

Arriving in
the island

The importance of Antigua's fine natural harbours, and its key position with regard to the main trade routes by sea to and from North America and Europe, were recognised from the earliest days of its settlement. In more recent times the combination of geographical location and a terrain suitable for the construction of an international airport has added to the island's importance. Antigua is now the focal point of a complicated network of air communications in the eastern Caribbean. There are daily flights to nearly all the other islands in the eastern Caribbean, as well as to New York (3½ hours) and Miami (2½ hours), with several flights each week to London (8 hours) and Toronto (4½ hours). The island is four hours behind Greenwich Mean Time and one hour ahead of Eastern Standard Time. There are five ports of entry into Antigua. St John's Deep Water Harbour caters for cruise ships and commercial shipping, and three much smaller ports are used by the numerous yachts which visit the island. The one which will be used by the majority of visitors, and certainly by nearly all those intending to stay for more than one day, is the airport.

V.C. Bird International Airport

The airport is situated on the north-eastern side of the island about four miles from St John's. It has one 9000 foot runway capable of operating all types of aircraft, including wide-bodied 'jumbo' jets and the Concorde supersonic airliner. The new terminal building which was opened in 1981 provides some of the

Unloading produce for the quayside market, St John's

most modern airport facilities in the region. The airport handles nearly 46 000 aircraft movements each year, of which well over half are scheduled flights. The island is served by Air Canada, American Airlines, British Airways, BWIA International and Eastern Airlines, along with one or two regional carriers. The local airline LIAT (owned jointly by the Governments of Antigua, Barbados, Dominica, Grenada, Guyana, Jamaica, Montserrat, St Kitts, St Lucia, St Vincent, and Trinidad & Tobago) is based in Antigua. It serves a total of twenty-four islands between Puerto Rico and Trinidad, with routes to Venezuela and Guyana. One or two small air charter companies are also based at the airport.

Accommodation

The visitor intending to stay for more than one day is required to give an address before leaving the airport. The visitor should make the necessary arrangements for accommodation before leaving his country of origin, unless he is prepared to be delayed on arrival. To assist in planning a vacation or business trip the Antigua Tourist Board has offices in Canada, Great Britain and the USA.

Antigua	Antigua Department of Tourism
	Thames Street, PO Box 363
	St John's
	Antigua
	Tel: 462-0029/462-0480
Canada	Antigua Department of Tourism & Trade
	60 St Clair Avenue East
	Suite 205
	Toronto
	Ontario M4T 1N5
	Tel: 416-961-3085
Great Britain	Antigua Department of Tourism & Trade
	15 Thayer Street
	London W1
	Tel: 01-486-7073/6
USA	Antigua Department of Tourism & Trade
	610 Fifth Avenue
	Suite 311
	New York
	New York 10020
	Tel: 212-541-4117

The island offers a complete range of accommodation, from first class luxury hotels and private clubs, through many medium and low-priced hotels and guest-houses, to self-catering cottages, villas and apartments. There is suitable accommodation for every requirement and every pocket. In addition to the travel guidance and literature which can be obtained from the offices of the Antigua Tourist Board, the prospective visitor can obtain more detailed information on the individual hotels which belong to the Association from

Antigua Hotels and Tourist Association
Long Street, PO Box 454
St John's
Antigua
Tel: 462-0374

The rates quoted by the majority of hotels are based on the cost of accommodation without meals – European Plan (EP), or with breakfast and either lunch or dinner – Modified American Plan (MAP). The rates are subject to a ten per cent service charge, and also a six per cent Government tax. The revenue collected from the latter is used to develop the island's tourist facilities.

Immigration and Customs

Entry into Antigua is kept as simple as possible. Citizens of the USA and Canada need only produce some form of identification. A passport only is required by citizens of Great Britain, the British Commonwealth countries, Japan, the EEC countries and the CARICOM countries. Anyone else will need both a passport and a visa. A return or onward ticket is required by every non-national entering the country by air. All visitors arriving by air will be given an immigration form to fill in before arrival. The carbon copy of this will be stamped by the immigration officer, who will keep the original. The copy must be retained and surrendered at the airport on departure. A departure tax of US$6.00 (or EC$15.00) is levied on all visitors staying for more than twenty-four hours; except those from CARICOM countries for whom the rate is US$4.00 (EC$10.00).

Each adult is allowed to bring in two hundred cigarettes or fifty cigars or half a pound of pipe tobacco, together with one quart of wine or spirits and six ounces of perfume. The importation of any narcotics or so-called 'recreational drugs' is prohibited. Each visitor has to make a verbal baggage declaration, but all luggage is subject to Customs inspection.

Currency

The units of currency used in Antigua are dollars (EC$) issued by the Eastern Caribbean Central Bank. The denominations are notes worth one, five, ten, 20 and 100 dollars, and coins worth one, two, five, ten, 25 and 50 cents, and one dollar. The EC dollar is linked to the US dollar at EC$2,70 to US$1.00. US currency is accepted everywhere at the rate fixed by the Antigua Chamber of Commerce at EC$2.60 to US$1.00. Travellers' cheques are accepted by many hotels, restaurants and stores, as are the usual credit cards. British and Canadian currency notes, and those of some other countries, are freely changeable at banks at rates which are quoted daily. All foreign currency transactions attract a one per cent Government levy. The visitor, because of the widespread use of the US dollar, should pay particular attention to the prices quoted for goods and services and always verify which dollar – the US or EC – is being quoted.

Transport

There is no organised bus service, with numbered routes, scheduled departures and marked stopping places. Instead there are a few routes, connecting the outlying parts of the island with St John's, along which individual bus owner-operators ply for hire from about 5.30 a.m. until nightfall. For the visitor with no firm schedule and who is in no hurry, these offer an interesting way of

The Jolly Roger *off Antigua*

visiting some of the villages and meeting some of the villagers. In general the buses are reasonably comfortable and clean, and provide a decidedly cheap way of travelling. The alternatives are taxis or rented cars.

Taxis are available at all times in St John's and at the airport. They are also available at the Deep Water Harbour and at the major hotels during the hours when they may be needed. The majority are owner-operated and the drivers belong to an association which has controlled rates for the more popular trips and tours. Care should be taken to agree a fare with the driver (making sure about the currency being quoted) before starting any journey.

There are a variety of car rental firms. Vehicles can be rented through a combined bureau at the airport or from their individual premises in and around St John's. A local driving licence is needed. This can be arranged by the car rental company on presentation of a valid licence from the visitor's home country and payment of a US$12.00 fee. It must be remembered that, despite the number of left-hand drive vehicles to be seen, Antigua follows the British practice of driving on the left-hand side of the road. There is a general upper speed limit of forty mph throughout the island, except in St John's and the villages where it is twenty mph. As will become apparent very quickly some of the roads in Antigua leave much to be desired and these speed limits will *not* be found irksome. The visitor who wishes to see as much of the island as possible is stongly recommended to hire a vehicle with four wheel drive – of which there are many available. The majority of the minor roads and tracks are unmotorable in anything else.

In keeping both with the generally informal tenor of Antiguan life, and the stubborn streak of independence in the Antiguan character, a number of highly individual driving habits are to be found amongst local drivers. The visitor must not be surprised at, or lose his patience with, the driver of the car in front who stops to chat in the middle of the road, turns right without signalling, or who parks on the inside corner of a right-angled bend. What, in New York or London, would produce apoplexy and rage among other road users, in Antigua produces only friendly toots on the horn and waving of the hand. The visitor should be prepared to smile and conform.

Clothing

The sensible visitor will also conform to local habits when it comes to clothing. While there are no regulations, bye-laws or restrictions on what can or cannot be worn, the wearing of swimsuits, very short shorts or see-through clothing in public places is not appreciated. Summer sports and casual wear is quite acceptable everywhere, and increasingly by both day and night. Some hotels require men to wear a jacket and tie in the evening, or perhaps on one or two evenings each week, but dinner jackets and evening dresses are now things of the past. One tourist brochure states that in the hotels 'a chic tropical look is expected'. The visitor who takes this dictum, which is open to wide interpretation, to apply to the whole of her stay on the island will be the one who suffers no embarrassment and earns the most local approbation.

Many of the shops in St John's and in the hotels specialise in providing day and evening wear for both men and women, with clothing ranging from tee-shirts to exotic, hand-screened cotton dresses, blouses, skirts and shirts. The visitor from even the least tropic-like parts of the world should have little difficulty in acquiring a suitable wardrobe.

Entertainment

Evening entertainment for the visitor outside the major beach hotels is somewhat limited. The larger hotels provide some kind of regular nightly show, featuring steel bands, limbo dancers, calypso singers, dance troupes or keyboard performers. The standard varies and as the entertainers tend to move from one hotel to another throughout the week there is little point in the visitor going to another hotel 'to catch a show', as he may be accustomed to doing in other parts of the world. One or two of the superior hotels occasionally feature outside artistes for limited seasons, but their appearances are not advertised widely.

In and around St John's there are several discos which may appeal to some of the younger visitors. From time to time local amateur dramatic groups put on productions, usually at the small open-air theatre in the University Centre. As the majority of these

The internationally known reggae singer, Kumasi, in Antigua

tend to be plays performed in the local dialect they will be of interest only to the visitor with a finely attuned ear. There are casinos at the Halcyon Cove Hotel on Dickinson Bay, the St Charles Hotel in St John's, the St James's Club at Mamora Bay, and the Royal Antiguan Hotel at Deep Bay.

On the whole the level of evening entertainment is not high. The visitor who is not staying in one of the hotels providing its own may well find that she quickly falls into the widespread Antiguan habit of retiring shortly after the evening meal and waking at daybreak. There is more than enough entertainment and enjoyment to be found in the island during the daylight hours to make up for the lack of a sophisticated night-life. While possibly only the world-weary will affirm that one steel band sounds much like another, or that if you have seen one limbo dancer you have seen them all, both the seasoned traveller and the novice 'first-timer' alike will soon observe that Antigua by day is quite unique.

A limbo dancer performs the difficult trick of edging underneath a flaming bar

Investment and finance

Enough has been said about the island's economy for the reader to appreciate why the Government is anxious to improve and expand the industrial sector. In spite of the priority given to promoting tourism and diversifying agriculture, there is still a large unemployment problem and an urgent need to train young Antiguans in new and more technical skills. Because of the difficulty in finding enough local capital to create more opportunities, legislation has been enacted which offers attractive incentives to foreign investors prepared to set up industrial enterprises. This policy has been reasonably successful and the number of new industrial concerns has increased steadily, but there is still the need for more. The island's work-force has an excellent record, free of disputes and the 'us against them' attitude found in many other parts of the world. With this background, the fiscal incentives, the ease of setting up a new factory, and Antigua's excellent communications, the island is an attractive investment area. Further information is available from:

Antigua	Ministry of Economic Development Queen Elizabeth Highway St John's Tel: 462-0092
Canada	Antigua Department of Tourism & Trade 60 St Clair Avenue East Suite 205 Toronto Ontario M4T 1N5 Tel: 416-961-3085
Great Britain	Antigua Department of Tourism & Trade 15 Thayer Street London W1 Tel: 01-486-7073/6
Hong Kong	Government of Antigua & Barbuda Trade Commission 88 Queen's Road Suite 1102 Hong Kong Tel: 5-265345
USA	Government of Antigua & Barbuda Investment Promotion Service 821 UN Plaza TM 600 New York New York 10017 Tel: 212-754-2005

At the end of 1982 Antigua and Barbuda was established as an Offshore Financial Centre, similar to the Bahamas and the Cayman Islands. This permits offshore corporations, banks and insurance companies to be set up with the minimum of Government interference, tax-free guarantees and exemption from foreign currency controls or levies. Full information about the legislation and the process of establishing and maintaining a corporation can be obtained from:

The Ministry of Finance
Long and High Streets
St John's
Antigua
Tel: 462-1199

Real estate

In addition to those wishing to invest in industry, private investors who would like to own a house or develop an area of land are also welcomed. Many North Americans and Europeans already own property in Antigua, and add to the cosmopolitan life of the island. Any visitor will be impressed by the amount of construction work which is taking place, and has been over the last decade or more. For anyone interested in buying property there is a complete range available, from 'time-share' apartments to luxurious sea-front houses. The real estate business is to a large extent run on informal and decidedly amateurish lines. The reasonably astute outsider with the necessary capital, plenty of patience, and sound legal advice, should have little difficulty in finding a fine holiday or retirement home which is also a good investment.

Living and working in Antigua

The strong attraction for anyone wishing to live and work in Antigua, other than the superb climate, is that there is no personal income tax. For someone wishing to live on the island but not work this is immaterial, but before such a person can own land or property he must possess an 'alien's land-holding licence'. This is not that easy to obtain because of the long bureaucratic process through which any application goes. But, provided the proper qualifications are met and the correct procedure is followed – for which legal advice is essential – eventually it can be obtained.

A work permit is needed by anyone who is not a citizen who wants to work in Antigua. Provided there is no threat to the security of the State and that there is no Antiguan available to do the job for which it is requested, such a permit is readily granted. Anyone can apply for citizenship after establishing residency for seven years and meeting certain other criteria.

Public holidays

The following are observed as national holidays in Antigua and Barbuda:
New Year's Day
Good Friday
Easter Monday
Labour Day (first Monday in May)
Whit Monday
The Queen's Official Birthday (second Saturday in June)
Carnival Monday (first Monday in August)
Carnival Tuesday (first Tuesday in August)
Merchants' Holiday (banks and Government offices remain
    open) (first Monday in October)
Independence Day (1 November)
Christmas Day
Boxing Day (26 December)

Diplomatic representation

The following countries have diplomatic representation in Antigua:

Denmark	Hon Consul	PO Box 104
		High Street
		St John's
		Tel: 462-0183
France	Hon Consul	PO Box 231
		St John's
		Tel: 462-2301
Netherlands	Hon Consul	PO Box 195
		High Street
		St John's
		Tel: 462-0308

United Kingdom	Representative	British High Commission St Mary's Street St John's Tel: 462-0008
USA	Chargé d'affaires	United States Embassy Queen Elizabeth Highway St John's Tel: 462-3505
Venezuela	Chargé d'affaires	Venezuelan Embassy Cross Street St John's Tel: 462-1574
West Germany	Hon Consul	PO Box 1259 St John's Tel: 462-3174

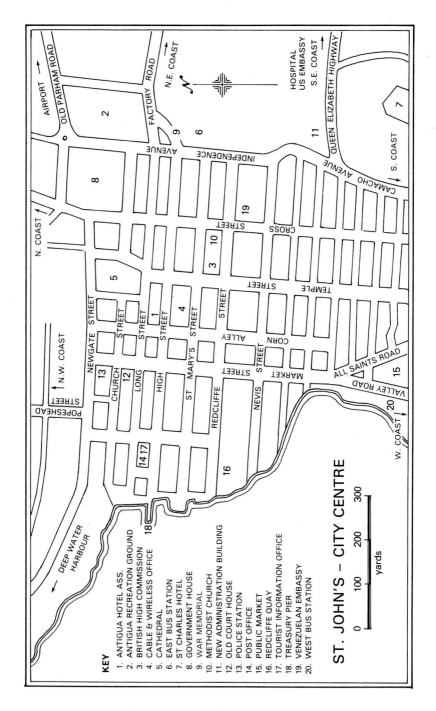

KEY

1. ANTIGUA HOTEL ASS.
2. ANTIGUA RECREATION GROUND
3. BRITISH HIGH COMMISSION
4. CABLE & WIRELESS OFFICE
5. CATHEDRAL
6. EAST BUS STATION
7. ST CHARLES HOTEL
8. GOVERNMENT HOUSE
9. WAR MEMORIAL
10. METHODIST CHURCH
11. NEW ADMINISTRATION BUILDING
12. OLD COURT HOUSE
13. POLICE STATION
14. POST OFFICE
15. PUBLIC MARKET
16. REDCLIFFE QUAY
17. TOURIST INFORMATION OFFICE
18. TREASURY PIER
19. VENEZUELAN EMBASSY
20. WEST BUS STATION

ST. JOHN'S – CITY CENTRE

yards
0   100   200   300

Chapter eight

The capital – St John's

The city of St John's sprawls all around the head of the large shallow bay which forms St John's Harbour. It has grown considerably since it was first laid out in the early 18th century, but particularly during the past twenty-five years or so. It now covers an area of about four square miles and embraces villages and communities which were once considered to be 'in the country', housing perhaps a third of the total population of the island. It also includes the deep water port facilities at the outer end of the peninsula which extends westwards into the middle of the harbour. The port is the first part of Antigua seen by about one third of all the visitors to the island. These arrive in the two hundred cruise ships which call each year. Although very few of these ships remain in port for more than one day their passengers add greatly to the life of St John's and to the economy of the country. During the months from November to May, when Caribbean cruising is most popular, the presence of two (and sometimes three or more) cruise ships in the harbour at the same time has an immediate impact on St John's. The main shopping streets are filled with tourists of all ages and speaking a variety of languages. The shopkeepers, taxi-drivers, tour bus operators and restaurateurs do thriving business, and the city becomes almost vibrant with noise and activity.

One regrettable feature of modern life and the supremacy of air travel is that it is now virtually impossible to travel between many of the islands of the eastern Caribbean by sea, other than in a cruise ship or a yacht. For anyone living in or visiting Antigua though the situation is not so bleak. A ferry service, using modern and very comfortable high-speed hydrofoils, operates daily (except

A colourful house in a side street of St John's

Sunday) to Montserrat, Guadeloupe and Dominica, with less frequent sailings to other islands such as St Kitts and St Martin. The ferry terminal is located at the lower end of High Street on the Treasury Pier, a small jetty which is also used as a berth for fishing boats, a landing place for yachtsmen, and a meeting place for some of the local waterfront characters.

The Deep Water Harbour

Before 1968 all ships bigger than the local inter-island craft had to anchor well outside the harbour. Passengers were then brought ashore in launches and landed at the Treasury Pier. Freight was landed in lighters and unloaded into warehouses around the harbour. All this changed when the present deep water port was constructed at the outer end of Rat Island, a small islet which was linked to the mainland by a causeway. The causeway was made much wider when part of the harbour was dredged to provide a turning basin off a wharf built on the southern side of Rat Island. To enable ships to reach the turning basin a channel well over a mile long was dredged through the bar across the mouth of the harbour. The port can now be used by ships of up to six hundred feet in length and drawing thirty or more feet of water. Some of the largest ships using the port are cruise ships. The Port Authority gives precedence to these over all other types of shipping in making berths available at the wharf. Cruise ship passengers can usually disembark within thirty minutes of the ship's arrival alongside.

Once ashore the passengers will find a tourist information desk inside the Port Administration Building – through which they have to pass in order to leave the port. Immediately outside there is a large shopping plaza with shops selling souvenirs, several bars and a couple of snack counters. International telephone facilities are also available. Taxis into the city, to a nearby beach, or for a tour of the island can be obtained from the stand situated between the Port Administration Building and the shopping plaza. A number of bus tours and excursions are available from the same place.

The road from the port into St John's crosses the original Rat Island causeway, now considerably widened. At the outer end,

Redcliffe Quay, St John's

nestling up against what used to be the eastern end of Rat Island when it was an island still, is Antigua's only rum distillery. This produces the island's famous 'Cavalier' rum. For anyone interested in the processes of its production a tour of the distillery can be arranged at reasonably short notice by contacting the manager (telephone 462-0458). Those who are more interested in sampling the product need travel no further than the nearest bar, hotel or restaurant. Rum, which has been termed 'the elixir of the islands', comes in many varieties, and there are dozens, if not hundreds, of different kinds throughout the Caribbean. While it may not be totally true to claim that Antigua's particular brand actually prolongs life, it certainly has excellent restorative qualities; no visitor who is not a teetotaller should leave the island without sampling it.

A little further along the road between the port and the city centre there is the chance to see local craftsmen at work in the various small boatyards which line the northern side of the harbour. Normally anything up to five or six boats of differing sizes will be found on stocks alongside the road. Regardless of size they are all built to a traditional design, without reference to any drawings and mostly with the use of hand tools. In the harbour behind them are bound to be seen some of the finished products at anchor, and it will be seen that the high, raked bows, the thick, stumpy mast and the after deck-house are repeated in craft ranging from 30 to 60 or 70 feet in length. The construction of these boats, like so much else in the modern world, is a dying art. They continue to be built in Antigua, but for how much longer in competition with boats made of steel and glass-reinforced plastic is open to question.

The city centre

The central area of St John's, containing the main shopping streets, banks and commercial institutions, is more or less confined to the limits of the original 18th century town. It appears today, allowing for changes in methods of transportation, still very much as it was described in the 1840s by Mrs Lanaghan.

The town, which is well arranged, covers a space of about 150 acres of land: most of the streets are wide and well-kept, and intersect each other at right angles – the principal ones running in a straight line down to the sea. There is one peculiarity attending the construction of these streets, which is, that there are no causeways; and consequently the pedestrian traveller has to elbow his way amid trucks and handbarrows, gigs, carriages and horsemen . . .

At the corners of the different streets are seated hucksters . . . some with their shallow trays, containing cakes of all descriptions, parched ground nuts, sugar cakes, and other confections, and varieties of fruit and vegetables; others have piles of cottons, coloured calicos, bright-tinted handkerchiefs, etc, placed by them, or carefully spread along the sides of the most frequented streets, to attract the eye of the passer-by.

While a good deal of rebuilding has taken place over the years, much of the old town still remains with plenty of wooden or stone buildings which the sharp-eyed Mrs Lanaghan, were she still alive, would have no trouble in recognising. In spite of the ever-increasing number of functional concrete buildings which are being erected in the main streets, they still contain some fine examples of early and mid-19th century architecture. To add to the charm and individuality of the city many of the older and better designed buildings are still private dwellings, ranging from large, two-storied houses to tiny one-or two-roomed cottages. Each has its garden, usually hidden behind a wall or fence, but seemingly overflowing with flowering shrubs and trees. Even in the very heart of the business section there are small shops and houses overshadowed by enormous mango, breadfruit and coconut trees.

Almost everything needed by the visitor in the way of goods and services, as well as cheap accommodation in small hotels and guest-houses, can be found within the area of the original town. All the main places of historical interest are in the same area and within easy walking distance of each other. The large complex of duty-free shops, offices and apartments on the waterfront was opened in 1988. It forms part of a scheme to redevelop the whole of the shoreline of the inner harbour in conjunction with a project to provide more alongside berthing arrangements for cruise ships.

Shopping

Shopping in St John's generally is not cheap, but the shopper who is prepared to spend some time looking around will usually be able to find a good buy. There are shops selling such things as fine china, crystal, Irish linen and Scottish woollens, together with one or two custom jewellers, and endless stores selling clothes of every kind. Items such as perfume, watches and cameras can be found, but possibly selling at prices not much different from those in North America. There is a wide range of local goods and handicrafts on sale, including ceramic ware, *Warri* boards and wooden carvings, straw and basket work, and costume jewellery made from shells, coral and polished stones. A few local artists, working very much in the highly colourful 'primitive' style, display their work on street corners or in small galleries. The local

'Cavalier' rum and indeed all liquor is cheap and plentiful, and the appropriate number of bottles of a favourite spirit may well make the best, if regrettably only transitory, souvenir of a stay in Antigua.

Business hours

The normal business and commercial life of the island takes place between 8.00 a.m. and 4.00 p.m. daily from Monday to Friday. Most shops and a few offices are open on Saturdays until midday, while some shops – particularly in Market Street – remain open all day. In years gone by all shops closed on Thursday afternoon (a colonial manifestation of the 'early closing day' beloved of English shopkeepers), but this is no longer widely observed. Although on Thursdays it is noticeably quieter in St John's there are plenty of shops which are open all day and business taking place. Banking hours are generally from 8.00 a.m. to 2.00 p.m. from Monday to Thursday, with an extension to 4.00 p.m. on Friday. One or two banks open for slightly longer hours.

Antigua's overseas telephone system is operated by Cable & Wireless, and provides facilities for direct dialling to the rest of the world. Public international telephone, telex, cable and facsimile facilities are available at the Cable & Wireless office on St Mary's Street. This is open seven days a week (Monday to Friday from 7.00 a.m. to 10.00 p.m., Saturday from 7.00 a.m. to 2.00 p.m., and Sunday from 4.00 to 8.00 p.m.). The main Post Office is at the western (lower) end of High Street, and is open daily from Monday to Friday between 8.00 a.m. and 4.00 p.m. The State issues many (for the pedantic philatelist probably too many) interesting and colourful postage stamps, and sets for collectors are available from the Philatelic Bureau in the Post Office.

Food and drink

Antigua is not renowned for its cuisine. There are no local dishes or foods which cannot be found in many other West Indian islands, even though perhaps prepared or served in slightly different ways. This is not to say that the local food is without interest or attraction. While 'kiddie (goat meat) stew' or 'shark quiche' (recipes for both of which are given in local cookery books) may not have more than minority appeal, there are many dishes which the visitor would be well advised to sample, given the opportunity. In St John's there are several restaurants which serve a variety of local dishes as alternatives to the ubiquitous hamburgers, steaks and 'french fries' of the average tourist-orientated menu. The visitor should have little difficulty in finding them, as they all advertise widely and are well sign-posted. No attempt is made here to indicate the specialities or attractions of any of them. The would-be patron is advised to seek local opinion about their relative merits as one good way of getting to know Antiguans.

Some of the dishes to look out for are:

Souse This is boiled pork (pig's head, knuckles or some other cut) marinated in water and lime-juice with onions, hot and sweet peppers, garlic and cucumber. It is usually served with lettuce and tomatoes and eaten with hot bread rolls.

Salt fish This is the traditional Antiguan Sunday morning breakfast dish. It is dried cod which has been soaked, boiled and boned, in a rich onion and tomato sauce. As a breakfast dish it is usually served with crushed aubergines (known locally as 'antrobers'). If eaten as a midday meal it is usually accompanied by **Doucouna**. This is a small pudding made from grated sweet potato and coconut mixed with flour and spices and boiled in a banana leaf.

Pepper Pot This is a rich, thick stew containing salt beef, pork, pumpkin, paw-paw, spinach, peas, aubergines and okras, with onion, garlic and spices. It can be served with dumplings or with a cornmeal pudding known as **Fungee**.

Conch Stew Another excellent stew prepared with the large shellfish called conch. The meat has to be tenderised before being cooked with onions, tomatoes and spices, but if done properly the result is delicious.

Although Antigua's cuisine may fail to excite the gourmet, the range of vegetables available to supplement the more international fare of the hotels and restaurants is very wide and well worth his attention. Besides those mentioned above, the island also produces corn, carrots, beans, yams, squash, eddoes, christophenes, cassava, dasheen, avocado pears, breadfruit and plantains. Once again, as with the local fruit, modern catering methods and the trend towards a stereotyped 'international' menu will prevent many of these from being offered in the average restaurant or hotel dining room. The hotel guest or restaurant customer who does find things such as fried aubergine, paw-paw *au gratin*, pumpkin fritters, candied sweet potato or scalloped plantain on the menu will know that she has chosen well.

With regard to drinks, once again Antigua has no speciality or concoction peculiar to the island. Rum has already been mentioned, and there can be few tourists who are not familiar – at least by name – with the more popular cocktails and mixtures which use rum as a base. Around Christmas time a deep red, non-alcoholic drink called **Sorrel** is prepared from the dried sepals of the sorrel flower. This is sweet and refreshing, and should never be refused if offered. The island grows plenty of lime trees and fresh limes are available at most times of the year. A lime squash made with fresh lime juice is an excellent thirst-quencher. Any attempt to serve a lime squash made from a commercially-bottled concentrate, which tastes totally different, should be rejected out of hand.

Places of interest

In recent years the change in appearance of St John's brought about by the construction of undistinguished concrete buildings has been combated to some extent by the careful renovation of some of the older buildings. **Redcliffe Quay**, at the lower end of Redcliffe Street, is a good example of this sort of restoration work. What used to be a collection of disused and decrepit warehouses has been transformed into a very attractive complex of shops, offices and eating places around a pleasant courtyard. In nearby St Mary's Street the **central Methodist church**, which was badly damaged by an earthquake in 1974, has also been lovingly repaired and restored to its original condition. Surrounded by well-kept lawns and with an imposing row of royal palms on the southern side it is now, just as Mrs Lanaghan described it soon after it was

The Cathedral Church of St John the Divine

built, '... an excellent building, superior to anything of the kind I have seen in the West Indies, and makes a good and commanding outward appearance, particularly when lighted up of an evening ...'

When these words were written the building which now dominates the city had not yet been built. The present day visitor cannot fail to see the twin spires and their silvery cupolas of a large grey church on a rise near the north-eastern end of the central part of St John's. This is the **Cathedral Church of St John the Divine**. Besides being the mother church of the Anglican Diocese of Antigua it is also considered to be a national monument with a meaning for the whole community. It is probably also the most imposing of all the Anglican cathedrals in the West Indies. Built in 1847, after the previous church on the site had been destroyed by an earthquake four years earlier, it has withstood subsequent earthquakes but suffered much damage. Like so many other such buildings throughout the world it requires constant repair and restoration work, for which there are never sufficient funds. The Cathedral is built of cement-washed stone but the interior is completely encased in pine to lessen the effects of damage by earthquake or hurricane. It can seat about two thousand people and congregations of this size are seen from time to time on State occasions or when a service is attended by royalty or high Anglican dignitaries. The life-sized metal figures on the pillars of the south gates to the churchyard were erected in 1789. They represent St John the Baptist and St John the Divine, and it is probable that they were taken from a French ship captured during the Seven Years War of 1756-63.

The oldest building still in use in St John's is the **Old Court House** at the junction of Long Street and Market Street. It was built in 1747 of stone quarried from one of the small islands off the north coast. Although it has been damaged, rebuilt and restored on several occasions since it still retains much of its original appearance. Once again the description given in *Antigua and the Antiguans* serves very well for today.

The court house is a very noble-looking pile for a West India colony, and indeed would not disgrace the boasted streets of London. The plan of the structure is very uniform and neat ...

The principal entrance (to the south) is approached by iron gates; and after crossing a small court-yard paved with large flag-stones, you enter a small corridor, supported by circular stone columns, with plain capitals. At each end of this corridor, a flight of stairs leads to the upper apartments in the east and west wings
. . .

The upper floor now houses the National Archives. These are not very extensive; most of the documentary history of Antigua resides abroad, either in official British government records or in the family papers of descendants of various plantation owners. However, the documentation which remains is now being gathered, catalogued and stored under proper conditions. Antigua's long history as a colony is also responsible for the meagre content of the museum on the ground floor of the court house. Many of the more valuable and important artefacts of the type normally displayed in national museums have long since left the island, or simply been allowed to deteriorate in the hands of those not conscious of their historical value. In spite of this the museum has acquired a considerable number of curiosities, displayed in such a way as to give the visitor a rather whimsical but none the less fascinating look at the history of Antigua. It is open daily from Monday to Friday.

About a quarter of a mile from the court house, at the eastern end of Long Street, is the **Antigua Recreation Ground**. Since 1981 this ground has been recognised as a venue for cricket Test matches. (A 'Test' match is a game in a 'Test series', played between teams representing countries which belong to the International Cricket Conference.) Any visitor who is in Antigua while one of these matches is being played is advised to see at least one day's play. Cricket is the game which has been described as a dramatic spectacle more akin to the theatre, ballet and the dance than a mere sporting activity. It is one which is closely linked with England and the English way of life; but it is one which has been mastered in no mean fashion by West Indians.

It is possible to argue (and many have done so: just as a game of cricket takes longer to play than any other, commentators on the game tend to be the most long-winded and dogmatic of sports writers) that no one from a non-cricket playing country can understand the finer points of the game (and for the uninitiated there are many . . .). This will not prevent anyone from getting a lot of enjoyment from watching a Test match in Antigua. Fellow spectators will be voluble, knowledgeable and above all friendly. There will be much noise, colour and amusement, and a great deal of entertainment from the players and onlookers alike. In addition the setting for such a game is superb. Despite its rather pedestrian name the Antigua Recreation Ground is in surroundings at least equal in attractiveness to Test match grounds with more appealing names, such as the Queen's Park Oval in Port of Spain or Sabina Park in Kingston. The ground is almost surrounded by trees and the lovely view through and over them to the south from the main stands adds greatly to the overall spectacle.

The ground is used also for soccer matches and occasional athletic meetings, but for two weeks each year all sporting activity ceases and it is transformed into 'Carnival City'.

Carnival

The annual carnival is the most popular cultural event in the island, appealing to visitors as much as it does to Antiguans. It takes place at the end of July, lasting for about ten days and ending with national holidays on the first Monday and Tuesday in August. It originated as a form of Christmas celebration. In days gone by from Christmas Eve until New Year's Day revellers took to the streets in weird costumes made from dried banana and other leaves, dressed as ghosts, or walking on stilts. After 1957, when the first summer carnival was held, these soon disappeared and Christmas in Antigua is now very much as in any other part of the world. The summer carnival was modelled on the much bigger and more famous Trinidad Carnival, with steel bands leading troupes called 'Mas bands' through the streets. Each troupe had its own theme with the members (who 'play Mas') dressed to depict things like 'The Glory of Ancient Rome', 'Aztecs', 'Mexicans' or 'Flags of Siena'. In later years they chose more topical or symbolic themes – 'Space People', 'Bird People', 'Our African Heritage' and the like. Today the emphasis is on fantasy or historical themes.

For the first five years after 1957 Carnival remained a purely

75

Carnival

local event, consisting of the street festivities together with a Carnival Queen contest and a calypso competition. In 1962 a Caribbean Queen contest was introduced which has since become the highlight of the many shows, attracting contestants from all parts of the West Indies. Today the Antigua Carnival embraces the Caribbean and local Queen contests, calypso and steel band competitions, a 'Miss Teenage Pageant', a junior calypso competition and a junior carnival. All these events are staged in 'Carnival City', where a large floodlit stage covers the cricket pitch, but a great deal of carnival activity goes on in other parts of St John's as well.

The original 1957 calypso competition had seven competitors for the title of 'Calypso King'; today the number is likely to be seventy or more. The final contestants are chosen from among the winners of preliminary competitions which are held in several 'calypso tents' around the city, established well before the opening of Carnival City. Steel bands made their appearance in Antigua shortly after the end of the Second World War. There was much local opposition at the time to 'pan men' and their music. This was overcome with the support of Lord Baldwin, a benevolent British Governor of the late 1940s. The unique sound of the steel band (now of course synonymous with the West Indies) has been heard in Antigua ever since. Each band taking part in the competition has its own 'pan yard' in which to tune up and practise, and naturally in the period leading up to carnival these are in constant use.

The noise and general excitement then begin well before the official ten day period of carnival, but reach a climax on the morning of the first Monday in August, in what is known as *Jouve* or *J'ouvert* (a corruption of *jour ouvert*). This is when the main streets of St John's are jammed with people marching, shuffling and dancing ('jumping up') to the music of steel bands and brass bands. This begins at four o'clock in the morning and continues for perhaps four or five hours until the sun is well overhead. St John's then closes its shutters and the streets remain deserted until mid-afternoon. This is the time when the costumed 'mas bands' parade through the town to the stage in Carnival City for judging. The stalwart 'masquerader' will continue his enjoyment throughout that night and the following day, ending with a final street 'jump up' at 'Las lap' on Tuesday afternoon. By the time this ends the streets will be partially blocked by the huge steel trolleys on which the steel bands perform, littered with the colourful remains of abandoned carnival costumes, and it will be apparent that Carnival is over for yet another year.

A steel band

All roads lead to St John's . . .

Anyone spending some time in St John's is bound to see that there are some areas which look dilapidated and in urgent need of restoration – but no more and no less than in any other capital city. These parts are more than compensated for by the many well-maintained and brightly painted houses, cottages, shops and commercial buildings, interspersed with eating places set in secluded courtyards surrounded and over-hung by shady tropical shrubs and trees. During the weekdays the main streets are filled with activity and St John's is clearly the centre of life on the island. The main roads radiate from it, the airport is but four miles away, the main port is an integral part of it, and a good many people from the outlying villages come in daily to work in or around the city. At the weekend and especially on Sunday it is different. The streets are then twice as wide, with no parked cars. The private dwellings with their doors and windows open stand out from the shuttered shops and offices. The odd goat or chicken is seen crossing the road. The inner part of the harbour with yachts and boats at anchor, seen clearly at the lower end of the main east-west streets, seems to be much more part of the town. Under such circumstances St John's assumes the air of just another West Indian village, belonging very much to its inhabitants and not to the world at large.

While to stay in one of the small hotels or guest-houses in the capital may not be everyone's idea of a Caribbean vacation, the changing moods of the place – from cosmopolitan city to sleepy village – will have their appeal. This type of accommodation may also be an attractive proposition for someone planning to hike or travel by bus around the island. The prosaically named East and West Bus Stations are less than half a mile apart on opposite sides of the city centre. The East Bus Station is used by buses carrying passengers to villages to the north and east, and the West Bus Station by those servicing the central, south and west communities.

Because St John's is the focus of the island's road network, and there is no road which follows all the way around the coast, anyone wishing to visit any part of the island is almost bound to take the city as a starting point. The next four chapters give a description of Antigua, working in a clockwise direction from St John's. The route of a suggested tour is indicated on the map which accompanies each chapter.

Chapter nine

Developed Antigua

The northern part of Antigua, that area to the north of a line drawn between St John's and Parham, is where the main development of the island has taken place in modern times. It contains not only the airport and the main sea port, together with the majority of Antiguan industries, but also well over half of all the visitor accommodation available on the island. There is also a lot of residential development, ranging from low-cost Government housing estates to expensive private houses set in their own landscaped grounds. As might be expected there is an extensive road network in this part of the island, including a road around most of the coastline. While much of the coast, away from the stretch facing the north-west, has no particular merit, some of the views to seaward – especially over North Sound – are very fine. A tour around the northern coast is recommended for these as much as the opportunity to see something of modern Antigua before venturing further afield.

The north-west coast, between the entrance to St John's Harbour and **Boon Point** (the northernmost point of Antigua), is undoubtedly the main tourist area on the island. It has three of the finest beaches. Two of them are lined with hotels, condominium developments, guest-houses and beach cottages, mixed with a few restaurants and beach bars, and there are other hotels and eating places a little way inland. The actual coastline remains attractive and relatively unspoiled. None of the buildings is obtrusive and they are all set in well-landscaped surroundings with plenty of palms and flowering shrubs. A little way inland, a couple of miles to the north-east of St John's, is the island's only 18-hole golf course at the **Cedar Valley Golf Club**. This offers full facilities to

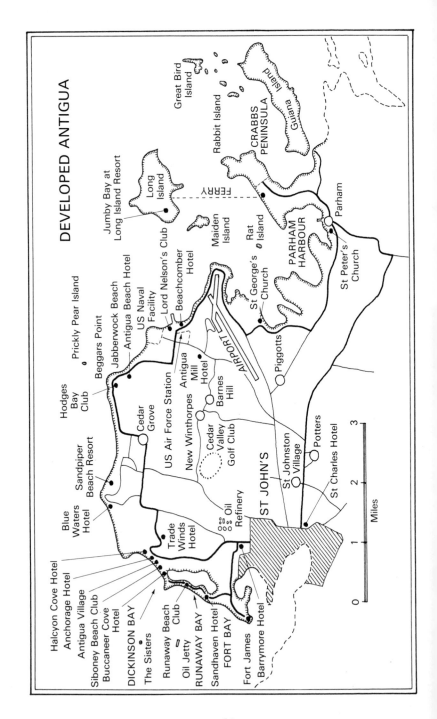

DEVELOPED ANTIGUA

Great Bird Island

Rabbit Island

CRABBS PENINSULA

Guiana Island

Jumby Bay at Long Island Resort

Long Island

FERRY

Maiden Island

Rat Island

Parham

PARHAM HARBOUR

St Peter's Church

Prickly Pear Island

St George's Church

US Naval Facility

Beggars Point

Jabberwock Beach

Antigua Beach Hotel

Lord Nelson's Club

Beachcomber Hotel

Piggotts

AIRPORT

Hodges Bay Club

Cedar Grove

Antigua Mill Hotel

New Winthorpes

Barnes Hill

US Air Force Station

Cedar Valley Golf Club

St Johnston Village

Potters

St Charles Hotel

ST JOHN'S

Sandpiper Beach Resort

Blue Waters Hotel

Oil Refinery

Halcyon Cove Hotel

Anchorage Hotel

Antigua Village

Siboney Beach Club

Buccaneer Cove Hotel

DICKINSON BAY

The Sisters

Runaway Beach Club

Oil Jetty

RUNAWAY BAY

Sandhaven Hotel

FORT BAY

Trade Winds Hotel

Fort James

Barrymore Hotel

0   1   2   3
Miles

82

visiting golfers. The third beach, behind which no development has taken place as yet, is the one closest to St John's. Called Fort Bay it begins in the south at Fort James.

Fort James and Fort Bay

To reach **Fort James**, situated on the promontory which forms the northern entrance point to St John's Harbour, leave the city by the aptly named Fort Road and continue northwards to the **Barrymore Hotel**. Turn left at the hotel and continue along the road until it reaches the sea. The road then runs parallel to the beach until it ends at the fort. Built in the first half of the 18th

Fort James

century to guard the harbour, Fort James had accommodation for about seventy men. The guns they were there to man were never very many, and were never fired in anger. Perhaps because of the lack of action a custom grew up whereby the officer commanding the fort began to extract dues from ships using the harbour. This practice, of dubious legality, was greatly resented by the local ship-owners but seems to have continued until well into the 19th century. The walls are still in excellent condition and a few of the cannon remain in place, but the main attraction of a visit is the excellent view it affords of the harbour and its approaches.

The beach in **Fort Bay** is equally excellent. There are lots of shady trees, especially at the back of the stretch nearest the fort, and a couple of small beach bars. It has long been the local beach for the residents of St John's and a few inhabitants swim there each morning throughout the year. While it is very popular with Antiguans on public holidays, particularly on Labour Day, for most of the year it is unusual to find more than one or two dozen people along its whole length.

Runaway Bay and Dickinson Bay

The next beach to the north in **Runaway Bay** will probably have a few more people using it on the average as it is lined with tourist accommodation of one sort or another. The buildings stand on a narrow strip of land separating the sea from one of the large salt ponds. The structure in the sea about a mile offshore is a jetty used for the transfer of oil fuel. It is connected by an underwater pipeline to the storage tanks which form part of the disused oil refinery on the inland side of the salt pond. The pond, which is called McKinnons, has a large population of migratory shore birds, terns, plovers and herons, in the fall. The road between it and the beach leads to the southern end of the next bay.

The beach in **Dickinson Bay** is the most popular of the three on this coast. There are four hotels, including two of the largest on the island, the **Halcyon Cove Beach Resort** and the **Anchorage**. The. is also a large condominum development called **Antigua Village**, several beach restaurants, and a number of water sports' centres. The bay provides ideal conditions for board-sailing, water-

*Dickinson Bay on the west coast of the island. The signpost says, London:
4076 miles*

skiing and snorkeling, as well as very safe swimming conditions on
a gently shelving beach. While it is understandably popular the
beach is never overcrowded.

Dickinson Bay is also used as the starting point for several boat
trips and tours. These include a 'pirate cruise' in the *Jolly Roger*, a
large wooden schooner, and a sailing cruise in a converted wooden
trawler called the *Servabo*. Both vessels provide substantial meals,
free drinks and a great deal of fun, with an opportunity for
swimming and snorkeling in Deep Bay (see Chapter 12) about one
hour's sailing from Dickinson Bay. Alternatively, there is a cruise
in a smaller boat around the north coast which includes a picnic,

swimming and snorkeling at Great Bird Island – one of the small islets off the north-east coast – or just a straightforward two-hour trip in a glass-bottomed boat. All of these tours are available on most days of the year. The necessary arrangements can be made on the spot, through hotels or travel agents, or at individual booking offices in St John's.

The north coast

The road around the north coast from Dickinson Bay crosses Marble Hill and then runs parallel to the coast about half a mile inland to the village of Cedar Grove. From there it follows the coastline to the airport. The area between Boon Point and Beggars Point is of no great interest to the visitor, being almost entirely residential and with no access to the one or two small beaches. About half a mile off Beggars Point is a very small treeless islet called **Prickly Pear Island**. This has a very fine beach on its western side. An enterprising Antiguan runs picnicking and swimming trips to it from a landing place on Beggars Point which is seen easily from the road. The beach to the south of Beggars Point and immediately alongside the road is known locally as the **Jabberwock Beach**. It offers good bathing and snorkeling under normal conditions, but occasionally the prevailing wind can stir up waves which may make it unsafe for small children.

The road meanders inland from the southern end of Jabberwock Beach and around the perimeter of the US Naval Facility. This was set up in 1956 in order to carry out oceanographic research, but is now a training establishment. It is adjacent to a small US Air Force Base which opened in 1957 as a missile and satellite tracking station. It now functions as a tracking station and communications centre. Both of these US Facilities occupy small areas of the total amount of land which was leased to the USA in 1941. During the Second World War the US Army Base covered several hundred acres and included all the land now occupied by the present airport.

The airport is constructed on the same site as the first airstrip, then called Coolidge Air Field, laid down by the then US Army Air Force in 1941. It was *not* named, as many local people seem to believe, after one of the less distinguished Presidents of the USA. Instead it was named in honour of a First World War hero – Captain Hamilton Coolidge of the US Army Air Corps who was killed in action over France in 1918. It was renamed in 1985.

The road around the airport passing Barnacle Point provides splendid views across Parham Sound to Long Island, Maiden Island and Crabbs Peninsula. On the southern side of the airport, after passing a quarry, the road divides, with the left-hand track leading to **St George's church** on Fitches Creek Bay. This is an Anglican church built in 1687, but remodelled into its present form fifty years later. Although in need of some restoration work, especially in the surrounding graveyard, it is in a very quiet, rural setting which exudes peace and tranquillity.

Parham, Crabbs Peninsula and North Sound

From St George's church an unpaved road leads around the head of Fitches Creek Bay and continues into the town of **Parham**, one of the original settlements of the 17th century. Because one of the early Governors lived there a common misconception has arisen that Parham was the original capital of Antigua. This was never the case, and although Parham used to be a port it never rivalled St John's. There is still a small pier at the eastern end of the town, and Parham Harbour provides a well-protected anchorage for yachts and small fishing boats, but there is no evidence of any other port facilities. The most prominent building in the town is **St Peter's Anglican Church**. It is octagonal in shape and has been described as being of great distinction, and of equally great significance to the ecclesiastical architecture of the British colonial period. Recent restoration work has made it possible for the layman to appreciate the distinction of the building, but it is difficult to believe that its importance to the architectural heritage of the island is fully recognised by either the lay or ecclesiastical authorities.

Crabbs Peninsula, which is low and flat, forms the eastern side of Parham Harbour. During the Second World War it was leased to the USA and housed a US Naval Air Station and a US Marine Corps Camp. Today it is the site for, among other things, a small

Great Bird Island

yacht marina and boat yard. The outer end of the peninsula is a restricted area used by the Antigua Defence Force. **Long Island**, about two miles away, houses the **Club at Jumby Bay**. A private ferry service is operated to and from the mainland, and visitors other than the Club's guests are welcomed provided arrangements are made with the management beforehand. The island is one of the places known to have been inhabited by both the Siboney people and the Arawaks. An archaeological site has been investigated on the north coast. In colonial times the island was a private estate mainly used for raising cattle.

On the eastern side of Crabbs Peninsula, and separated from the mainland by The Narrows, a stretch of water about four hundred feet wide, is the largest of Antigua's off-lying islands. **Guiana Island** acquired its name from its first settlers. These were some Englishmen who had been forced to leave Dutch Guiana (now Surinam) in 1667, after the Treaty of Breda left that country in Dutch hands. Originally it was planted with sugar cane, but under subsequent owners it became a shooting estate. During the years between the First and Second World Wars it was turned into a park, with avenues of trees, coconut groves and immense shrubberies and flower beds. In recent years it has been allowed to return to its natural state and is now a Nature Reserve, with a herd of deer and a flock of prize sheep. It is also a protected habitat of Guinea-fowl, wild ducks and other birds. A pontoon bridge connects it to the mainland, but there is no public access. Arrangements for visits by persons with specific interests can be made with the Ministry of Agriculture, but lots of advance notice is needed.

To the north of Guiana Island and lying amidst numerous patches of coral reef are several other, much smaller, islands. The largest, called **Great Bird Island**, is very popular with picnicking and swimming parties. It provides an ideal overnight anchorage for yachts on the western side. The eastern side of the island is an eroded limestone cliff nearly a hundred feet high. This provides good nesting for sea birds, and spectacular views of the surrounding reefs from the top. The island can be reached easily by means of one of the boats which run day tours from Dickinson Bay or other places on the west coast.

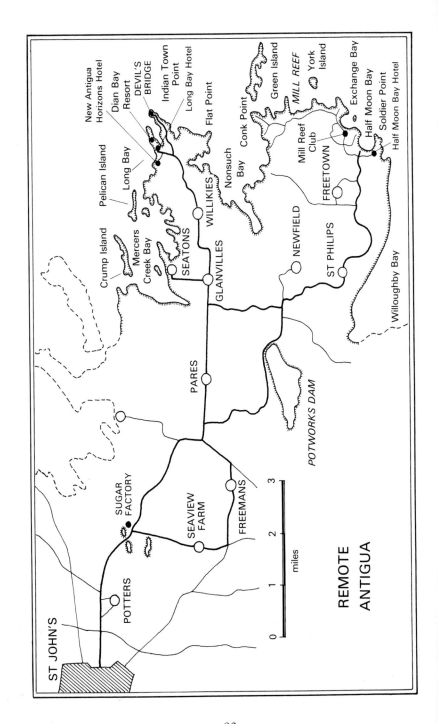

REMOTE ANTIGUA

Chapter ten

Remote Antigua

The eastern part of the island, between Mercers Creek Bay and Willoughby Bay, is shaped like the gigantic claw of a crab. It is not only the remotest part (if that term can be used in an island which is only fifteen miles across from east to west, and even less from north to south), in terms of distance from St John's, but it is the part which has the least to attract the visitor.

Mercers Creek Bay and Nonsuch Bay

In the early part of the last century Henry Coleridge in his book *Six Months in the West Indies* described the coastline of Antigua.

> . . . *indented in every direction with creeks and bays and coves, some of them running into the centre of the plantations like canals, some swelling into estuaries, and others forming spacious harbours. Beyond these an infinite variety of islands and islets stud the bosom of the blue sea, and stand out like so many advanced posts of defence against the invading waves. They are of all shapes and sizes.*

Allowing for the odd hyperbole this description applies particularly to the eastern side of the island. **Mercers Creek Bay** is almost totally enclosed, with narrow openings to the sea between small islets lying across the entrance. The shoreline is divided into small coves and creeks by narrow spits of land. A good panoramic view of the bay can be obtained from the bluff on which the village of **Seatons** is built. This small detour from the main road between St John's and the north-eastern point of the island is well worth making. The main road itself passes through the village of Willikies and ends at **Long Bay**, where there is another excellent bathing beach with a hotel at either end. This beach is very popular with Antiguans. At the weekend during the summer months (many local people resolutely refuse to enter the sea between about November and March, although the sea temperature never varies by more than three degrees about a mean of 79°F throughout the year) it may become a little crowded, but only in comparison to the normal conditions prevailing on Antiguan beaches.

Indian Town Point is the north-eastern extremity of the island. It is a low, flat area of mostly exposed and eroded limestone, reached by a track which passes through an arid stretch of countryside. This is probably the driest part of the whole island, as is borne out by the various species of cacti to be seen. The main attraction of the Point other than the views of the Atlantic is the natural limestone arch on the eastern side known as **Devil's Bridge**. This has been created by the action of the surf, and when the sea is running the formation of the arch produces some dramatic effects of waves and spray. Regardless of its name Indian Town Point is not the location of any 'Indian' or pre-historic settlement, and the origin of the name is obscure. Some evidence of Arawak habitation has been found in this part of the island, but the lack of an adequate rainfall undoubtedly would have prevented any permanent settlement.

To the south of Indian Town Point, between the open pincers of the 'crab's claw', is **Nonsuch Bay**. This is virtually inaccessible by public road. With no beaches or sites of historical interest around its shores it is of little interest to the general visitor. The bay is popular with yachtsmen although it is not easy to get into from seaward. A large coral reef lies across the mouth protecting it from the Atlantic swells. The main entrance is through a narrow channel from the south which passes between the mainland and the small islet called Green Island. The only other entrance is through a tortuous channel between the reefs from the north. The bay is supposed to have been named after a ship, the *Nonsuch*, which anchored there for some time in 1647, presumably the first ever to do so.

Devil's Bridge

Willoughby Bay and Half Moon Bay

To reach the area to the south of Nonsuch Bay from Indian Town Point it is necessary to return inland to the village of Glanvilles, and then take the road south to **St Philips**. This small village takes its name from the Anglican church which has been there since about 1690, and around which it grew up. It is built near the edge of the steep escarpment which forms the north shore of **Willoughby Bay**, and some superb views of the bay and the country on the opposite side are obtained at various points along the road which leads from the village to the east. The bay, in spite of its size, was never of any importance as a harbour. It is open to the prevailing wind and the entrance is almost completely blocked by coral reefs. These can be seen quite clearly from the road. Henry Coleridge described the view over the bay as 'one of the finest panoramic views of the world', and few of those who stop to admire it will disagree.

Half Moon Bay

Half Moon Bay, where the road ends, is equally useless as a harbour but is an outstanding tourist attraction. Due to its almost circular shape, with the entrance facing the Atlantic swells, every kind of sea state from crashing rollers to rippling wavelets is to be found at some point along the length of its beach, providing a wide variety of swimming conditions. **Half Moon Bay Hotel** on the south-western side not only has its own 9-hole golf course, but also a five court tennis complex in which several professional tournaments are played each year.

The area to the north of Half Moon Bay as far as the southern side of Nonsuch Bay, including all the small islands offshore, belongs to a proprietary club with limited membership, called the **Mill Reef Club**. This consists of a clubhouse on Exchange Bay and numerous elegant tropical houses scattered around its 1300 or so acres, together with a 9-hole golf course and a yacht harbour. The Club was started in 1948, and although some of Antigua's politicians and prominent citizens have been made honorary members, it was intended to be – and remains – an exclusive resort for in the main wealthy North Americans.

The creation of Mill Reef by an American architect so soon after the end of the Second World War helped to consolidate the connection between Antigua and the USA which the war had introduced. The construction work necessitated bringing an American building contractor to the island and created new employment opportunities. The requirements of the club members for goods and services of every kind helped to bring into being many new businesses, and introduced new American products and business methods to the island. Today Antigua benefits not only by the number of jobs provided by the club and the contribution the members make to the general revenue, but also from the charitable work carried out through the Mill Reef Fund, in the form of grants, donations and scholarships. The island also benefits from the free publicity it is given by the internationally known people who are members or guests of the club. In some circles, due to the foresight of its founder Mr 'Happy' Ward, Antigua is synonymous with the Mill Reef Club; just as in other circles, due to the prowess of Mr 'Vivi' Richards, it is synonymous with the game of cricket.

Potworks Dam and Sea View Farm

A visit to the east coast from St John's gives the opportunity of crossing the island by two different routes. It is suggested that the return trip is made via the island's main reservoir and two of the central villages. The reservoir which is always referred to as the **Potworks Dam** was created in the late 1960s, and is fed by streams which flow into it during rainy weather. It is very shallow and during times of severe drought virtually dries out. The road along the north side passes over the dam proper and there is an observation ·point at the western end. The reservoir has no intrinsic value as a tourist attraction, as its setting in the flattest part of the island is very dull. However the bird life which it harbours will be of interest to the bird-watcher.

From the reservoir the visitor is recommended to follow a route which leads through the village of Freemans to another small community called **Sea View Farm**. This has an excellent view of the sea to the north and north-west, but the amount of farming activity carried on around it hardly justifies the name. It is far more renowned for its potteries, and several will be found along the road running through the village. (The visitor should not be misled by the much larger community about two miles to the north-west, which is called Potters Village, but where in fact there are no potteries.) The potters, who are all female, make mostly charcoal braziers ('coal pots'), cooking pots and plant pots intended for local use. They also produce a range of smaller items which many visitors find make good souvenirs. All the pottery is a distinctive deep red in colour, and is fired in open pits behind the potters' houses. A visit to one of these potteries, the inspection of the products, and the negotiations about prices, are all carried out in a very informal way. Such a visit will also provide another insight into the ordinary village way of life.

The road northwards from the village leads back to St John's past the Sugar Factory. The factory itself is almost defunct, in spite of recent efforts to revive a small sugar industry to meet purely local needs. The various ponds in the vicinity are of interest to bird-watchers for the ducks and other waterfowl which breed and feed there.

Chapter eleven

Historic Antigua

The focal point of any visit to the south of the island must be English Harbour and its celebrated Dockyard. The harbour is one of the smaller indentations in the coastline of Antigua, but the security it has offered ships and boats throughout the island's history gives it an importance which far belies its size. The creation and development of a Naval Dockyard within the harbour had an effect on the whole of the surrounding countryside. Because of this there are several other aspects of this part of the island which are equally interesting and worth the visitor's attention.

Mrs Lanaghan described the road from St John's to English Harbour as, '. . . for the most part dull and uninteresting . . .' This was perhaps a little harsh; between the city and the outskirts of **Liberta** there is not much of interest, but after that, where the road winds over the hills, through Liberta and down to Falmouth, the scenery and views are most attractive. Neither need the journey be a dull one, provided the traveller has time to stop now and then to observe life in the villages and away from the road.

Monks Hill and Falmouth Harbour

At Liberta the road to **Monks Hill Fort** (properly called Great George Fort) is signposted. For those who wish to see one of Antigua's finest historical sites it is necessary to turn off the main road and head for the small village of **Table Hill Gordon**. From there it is about one mile to the fort. The track offers easy walking, but it is only motorable in a four wheel drive vehicle.

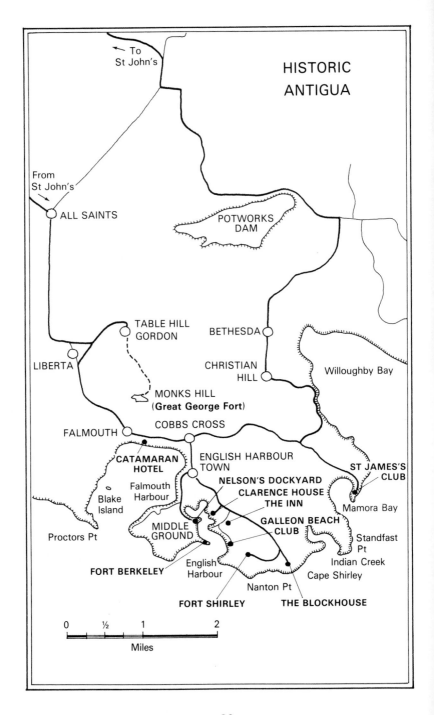

HISTORIC
ANTIGUA

← To
St John's

From
St John's

○ ALL SAINTS

POTWORKS
DAM

TABLE HILL
GORDON

BETHESDA ○

LIBERTA ○

CHRISTIAN
HILL ○

Willoughby Bay

MONKS HILL
(Great George Fort)

FALMOUTH ○

COBBS CROSS ○

ENGLISH HARBOUR
TOWN

CATAMARAN
HOTEL

NELSON'S DOCKYARD
CLARENCE HOUSE
THE INN

ST JAMES'S
CLUB

Falmouth
Harbour

GALLEON BEACH
CLUB

Mamora Bay

Blake
Island

MIDDLE
GROUND

Standfast
Pt

Proctors Pt

FORT BERKELEY

English
Harbour

Indian Creek

Cape Shirley

Nanton Pt

FORT SHIRLEY

THE BLOCKHOUSE

0   ½   1   2

Miles

The Catamaran marina at Falmouth Harbour

The fort, which was also intended to be a citadel in which non-combatants could take refuge, as well as a defensive position and signal station, was begun towards the end of the 17th century and completed in about 1705. The outer walls, which are more or less complete, embraced an area of over seven acres on which were built barracks, magazines, a hospital and two enormous cisterns. In the event it was never needed as a refuge, its guns were never fired, and after the end of the Napoleonic wars it soon fell into disuse except as a signal station. This does not detract from the incredible setting of the fort on top of a steep-sided hill dominating Falmouth Harbour and the surrounding countryside. While it is nowhere near as big, and certainly not anywhere near in the same state of repair, as the similar structures of Citadel-Henry in Haiti or Brimstone Hill in St Kitts, the siting of Great George Fort is just as impressive. The views from it are equally spectacular.

The track from Table Hill Gordon leads to the only entrance, an arched doorway on the north side, and continues inside towards the eastern end. The whole of the fort is overgrown with acacia bushes and cacti, and all the buildings are in ruins. Nothing much can be seen of the surroundings until the higher ground at the eastern end is reached. There, by moving a few paces one way or the other around the circular stone structure which was once the base of a flagstaff, it is possible to see out in every direction. The southern side of Monks Hill is precipitous and from the top of the wall at the south-eastern extremity of the fort, nearly seven hundred feet above sea level, the view is truly magnificent. This alone, the panorama of Falmouth Harbour, English Harbour, and the large peninsula called Middle Ground between them, makes the climb (or bumpy ride in a cross-country vehicle) very worthwhile. It is possible to descend by a track which leads down to the village of Cobbs Cross on Falmouth Harbour, but this is suitable only for walking.

Falmouth Harbour has been in use as a safe anchorage for ships since the earliest days, and Falmouth Town on the northern side was one of the first settlements. Today the village houses only a small community and any importance it had has long since been transferred across the bay to the town of English Harbour. The harbour itself remains very much in use, at times providing anchorages for as many yachts as English Harbour, from which it is separated by a narrow isthmus. The road from St John's passes through Falmouth and Cobbs Cross before reaching English Harbour Town. There it divides, with the right-hand road leading to the Dockyard, and the left-hand one leading to the remains of the fortifications which used to guard it. It is recommended that the latter are visited first, in order to get an overall view of English Harbour and to place the Dockyard in its proper perspective.

Shirley Heights

The extensive ruins of barracks, gun emplacements, magazines, and other military buildings found all over the high ground to the east of English Harbour are generally referred to as **Shirley Heights**. This title properly belongs to the bluff overlooking the

The ruined barracks at Shirley Heights

harbour on which are those ruins which comprise Fort Shirley. The road from English Harbour Town which climbs up the side of a hill passes first of all a complex called the Royal Artillery Quarters. A restored building contains a small museum and an information centre. From there the road runs along the crest of a ridge. It divides near a large cannon half-buried upright in the middle of the road. The left-hand road continues to climb until it ends on top of the cliff which forms **Cape Shirley**, well over four hundred feet above sea level. The buildings in this vicinity formed **The Blockhouse**, and consisted of barracks, officers' quarters, a magazine and various domestic quarters. Where there is now a large open space around a tall mast which supports a navigation light, a battery of guns was once mounted to protect the eastern and southern approaches to English Harbour. Blockhouse Hill provides a splendid view of the whole of the south-eastern coast. Immediately below the hill to the east is **Indian Creek**. This is one of the most important, and probably one of the first, sites inhabited by the Arawaks. This is next door to Mamora Bay and the prominent buildings of the **St James's Club** – one of the newest exclusive resorts in Antigua. Further away still in the east is Willoughby Bay, with a line of breakers showing up the reefs across its entrance. On a clear day the outline of the French island of Guadeloupe can be seen over forty miles away to the south.

The right-hand road from the half-buried cannon leads to **Fort Shirley**. This was named after General Sir Thomas Shirley, who was Governor of the Leeward Islands in Antigua from 1781 to 1791. During this period most of the fortifications above English Harbour were built. The fort consisted of the usual parade ground and officers' quarters, together with a hospital, canteen, signal station and of course a battery of guns. The ordnance building which was behind the gun emplacement has been converted into a restaurant, and instead of guns the gun platform now supports picnic tables. These overlook English Harbour from a height of nearly five hundred feet. The view, which must be one of the finest and most-photographed in the Caribbean, makes it easy to appreciate the excellence of the harbour and the importance of the Dockyard to the Royal Navy of two hundred years ago. From the same place Montserrat can be seen on most days, just over thirty miles away to the south-west. Redonda, further round to the west

St James's Club

Yachts and the jetty at St James's Club

and about forty miles away, can also be seen in the right conditions of visibility.

For those not content to sit at one of the outdoor tables and enjoy the view, within a few minutes' walk are the ruins of the military hospital. These are above **Nanton Point**, the southernmost tip of the island. Between the hospital and the rest of the fort there is a cemetery in a small valley. The various memorials and tombstones with inscriptions that are still legible show that yellow-fever and other tropical illnesses were the main dangers faced by soldiers in the West Indies in the 18th and 19th centuries. That the next greatest danger to health was the competence of the military physicians of the day is surely borne out by the proximity of the cemetery to the hospital.

Shirley Heights by Charles Jane is a handy guide to all the fortifications which surround the Dockyard. It contains a lot of interesting material about the men who manned them. It is on sale at the information centre, in the Dockyard and from shops in St John's. For anyone who visits Shirley Heights with an interest in things other than the marvellous views it is highly recommended.

Clarence House

Standing on a slope overlooking the inner part of English Harbour, and off to the left from the road leading from Shirley Heights back to English Harbour Town, is **Clarence House**. This is the official country residence of the Governor-General, although not often used as such. The house is a very fine example of the Georgian style of architecture adapted for the climate of the West Indies. When the Governor-General is not in residence it is opened to the public, and a visit is recommended. It was built in 1787 for the use of Prince William Henry, Duke of Clarence (later King William IV) who was then serving in the Royal Navy, and in command of a ship on the Leeward Islands Station. The house is still furnished and decorated very much in the style of the period. Both inside and out it appears much as it did when it was built.

Nelson's Dockyard

After having seen English Harbour both from Shirley Heights and the garden of Clarence House, one cannot fail to appreciate its excellence as a harbour, nor to understand why a Naval Dockyard was built there. The value of the harbour as a safe refuge from hurricanes was recognised from the beginning, but it was not until the start of the 18th century that it was used regularly by Naval ships. Fort Berkeley at the end of the narrow peninsula which forms the western entrance point was built by 1704, and by 1728 a small dockyard called St Helena had been constructed on the eastern side between Commissioners Bay and Freemans Bay (where there is now a commercial boat-yard). The present dockyard, which is the group of buildings and wharves on the western side, on Middle Ground, was started in 1743. Its development continued at intervals for another sixty years or so after that.

The Admiral's House in Nelson's Dockyard at English Harbour

The Dockyard is now always referred to as **'Nelson's Dockyard'**, although the famous British admiral was in no way responsible for its inception or development. His only connection with Antigua was while he was captain of a ship stationed in the Leeward Islands between 1784 and 1787. During this period he spent a considerable amount of time in English Harbour. From his letters he appears to have hated it, calling it a 'vile spot' and 'this infernal hole'. Throughout his time on the Leeward Islands Station Nelson seems to have had a special dislike of Antigua and its people. 'I am not very popular with the people,' he wrote. 'They have never visited me, and I have not set foot in any house since I have been on the station . . .'

That the Dockyard should now be named after someone who not only had nothing to do with its founding, but actually detested the place, could be considered to be more than a little unjust. However, with the establishment of the 'Nelson's Dockyard National Park', embracing the whole of English Harbour and Shirley Heights, the name has been given official sanction and is here to stay; an irritation perhaps only to the purist. On the other hand, the presence in the Dockyard of a 'Lord Nelson's Gallery' selling 'original native and contemporary works by local artists', and a teashop offering a 'home-made Nelson's Hero Sandwich', may well be thought by many who honour the 'Immortal Memory' as carrying the connection a little too far . . .

The Dockyard is approached along the road through **English Harbour Town** which skirts the eastern side of Falmouth Harbour. Having crossed the isthmus the road ends at the Dockyard gate. Cars are not allowed inside but ample parking space is provided near a long, low building which houses a bank, post office and many souvenir stalls. By walking along a track which runs outside the Dockyard wall, starting near the main gate, it is possible to reach the ruins of **Fort Berkeley**. This ten-minute stroll, if taken before looking at the Dockyard itself, will complete the overall look at English Harbour and its defences. It also provides close-up views of boats entering and leaving, much as they have been doing in different forms for the past three hundred years or more.

Inside the Dockyard there is a small museum with contents equally as varied and capricious as those in the St John's museum, but naturally orientated towards the sea and the Royal Navy. It is housed in an elegant, two-storied building known as the **Admiral's House** — in another attempt to link Nelson with the Dockyard; in fact it was built 50 years after his death.

The military garrison left Antigua in 1854, but the Royal Navy continued to use the Dockyard for another thirty-five years before it was abandoned in 1889. By that time the majority of naval vessels were too big to use the harbour and the Dockyard facilities were much too limited. In 1906 it was transferred to the Government of Antigua and from then on fell into complete disrepair. It was saved from total destruction only by the formation in 1951 of the Society of the Friends of English Harbour. This was founded by the then Governor, Sir Kenneth Blackburne, who recognised the historical importance of the Dockyard as well as the role English Harbour could play as a yachting centre. Funds were collected internationally to restore many of the buildings and in 1961 the Dockyard was 're-opened' very much in its present form.

Since then English Harbour has developed into one of the finest yacht harbours in the Caribbean. It has most of the facilities needed by yachtsmen either in the Dockyard buildings or across the harbour at St Helena. The revenue derived from the yachting industry goes in part to continue the historical renovation and preservation work. While the two activities are not totally compatible, the needs of modern yachts being what they are, a very reasonable balance has been achieved. The yachts at anchor or alongside the wharves, together with the activity going on in and around many of the buildings, add greatly to the ambience of the Dockyard. It is busier now, and particularly so during the cruising season, than ever it was during its days as a Naval Base. It is only right that Mrs Lanaghan should have the last word:

The dockyard presents a fine and noble appearance; and . . .
everything seems to be conducted in the best possible manner;
while the yard itself is kept so beautifully clean, that a walk
through it affords real pleasure.

Mamora Bay and Bethesda

After touring Shirley Heights and the Dockyard the return to St John's can be made by a road which begins by running to the east from **Cobbs Cross**. This eventually leads to the privately-owned **St James's Club** on Mamora Bay. This is an exclusive resort with its own restaurants, gymnasium, stables, tennis court complex and swimming pool. It also runs its own yacht club in the bay. Although the entrance is open to the east, the bay provides a calm anchorage for up to a hundred boats. The club can be visited by non-members on payment of a temporary membership fee for one day only.

From Mamora Bay the road follows the western coast of Willoughby Bay, winding through some pleasant scenery to the village of **Bethesda**. While today the village is no different from a dozen other villages in Antigua, Bethesda holds a special place in the history of the island. It grew up around the first school in the island, and possibly in the British West Indies generally, which taught slaves. This was opened in 1813 by a Mr and Mrs Thwaites of English Harbour Town, who gave it the Biblical name for a house of mercy, Bethesda. After the emancipation of slaves in 1834 houses began to be built around the schoolroom, and the community emerged as one of the first 'free villages'. From Bethesda the road leads around the eastern side of the Potworks Dam and so back to St John's.

Chapter twelve

Scenic Antigua

The south-western part of Antigua, with its steep-sided hills, picturesque villages and easily accessible, undeveloped coastline, is the most scenic portion of the island. A circular tour of this region is possible, starting and ending in St John's. It is recommended that this be taken in a clockwise direction, leaving the city by the All Saints Road.

Buckleys, Swetes and Bendals

Half way between St John's and All Saints the road divides. The right-hand fork runs southwards to the village of **Buckleys**. From there it runs along the crest of a ridge for about two miles to the village of **Swetes**. To the south-west there is a most attractive valley, with several small dams forming reservoirs which descend to the north-west. There is a road through this valley (which has no official name, although the road itself is referred to locally as 'Body Ponds' Road') beginning at the village of **Bendals**, a mile and a half to the west of Buckleys. This road provides an alternative way of reaching Swetes, but is only motorable in a cross-country vehicle.

Fig Tree Hill and Old Road

From Swetes the road is taken which leads to the west and directly into the hills. It rises and falls steeply through the village of John Hughes, meanders around **Fig Tree Hill**, and then descends to Old Road, the oldest settlement in the island. Of this part of the

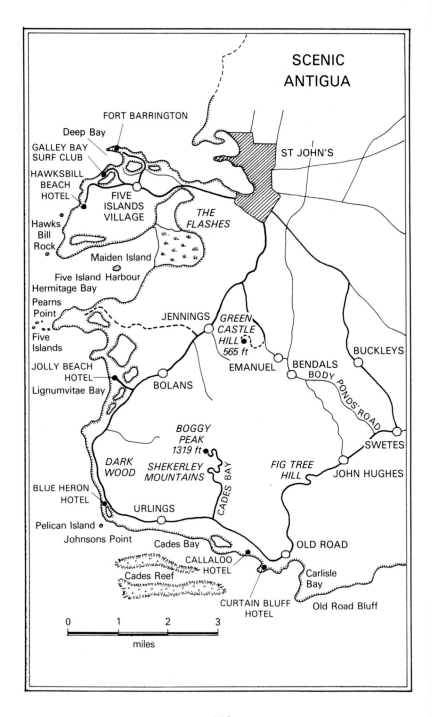

SCENIC ANTIGUA

FORT BARRINGTON

Deep Bay

GALLEY BAY
SURF CLUB

HAWKSBILL
BEACH
HOTEL

FIVE
ISLANDS
VILLAGE

Hawks
Bill
Rock

ST JOHN'S

THE
FLASHES

Maiden Island

Five Island Harbour

Hermitage Bay

Pearns
Point

JENNINGS

GREEN
CASTLE
HILL
565 ft

BUCKLEYS

Five
Islands

EMANUEL

BENDALS

JOLLY BEACH
HOTEL

Lignumvitae Bay

BOLANS

BODY
PONDS' ROAD

BOGGY
PEAK
1319 ft

SWETES

DARK
WOOD

SHEKERLEY
MOUNTAINS

FIG TREE
HILL

JOHN HUGHES

CADES BAY

BLUE HERON
HOTEL

URLINGS

Pelican Island

Johnsons Point

Cades Bay

CALLALOO
HOTEL

Cades Reef

OLD ROAD

Carlisle
Bay

CURTAIN BLUFF
HOTEL

Old Road Bluff

0   1   2   3

miles

110

tour around Fig Tree Hill the indefatigable Mrs Lanaghan wrote:

> ... *no description I have ever heard of it has sufficiently set forth its beauty. Upon one side of the road is a deep ravine, whose irregular descent is hidden by trees of every description, which cover it to the bottom, and again ascend upon the opposite bank, until they reach the top of the neighbouring mountain; on the other side are sloping hills, carpeted with the gayest emerald. This beautiful hill takes its name from several large fig-trees which grow around ...*

The wild fig trees are not much in evidence today but otherwise the description is perfect. As the road descends to Old Road the country becomes more open, with extensive pastures dotted with truly enormous mango trees on one side, and small banana groves on the other. Nearer to the coast there are some large coconut plantations and more extensive banana groves.

Old Road lies around the head of Carlisle Bay. The village acquired its name from the fact that, for the original settlers of 1632, **Carlisle Bay** offered a safe anchorage or 'road' (a common term of the early 17th century for a safe and sheltered anchorage) for their ships. Presumably, once Falmouth Harbour and then St John's Harbour started to be used the importance of Carlisle Bay decreased, and it became the 'old road'. This name then stuck to the settlement which had grown up there. Similar villages with the same name, now some distance from the main port, are found in St Kitts and Montserrat.

There is a fine beach at the head of Carlisle Bay, backed by a coconut plantation which provides plenty of shade. The village itself, which not surprisingly has the oldest church in Antigua, is very small, quiet and peaceful. At its western end, occupying the whole of **Curtain Bluff** is the hotel of the same name. This superbly sited resort has a beach on either side of the bluff, its own tennis court complex in which annual professional tournaments are played, and extensive facilities for sailing, fishing and water sports.

Boggy Peak

From Old Road the road follows the coast all the way around the south-western part of the the island. At **Cades Bay**, about two

Morris Bay near Curtain Bluff in the south of the island

miles from the village, there are several large fields of pineapples under cultivation in a small valley at the foot of the Shekerley Mountains. The road running northwards in this valley leads to the summit of **Boggy Peak**, the highest point of the island. A microwave communication station occupies the whole of the summit behind a substantial fence. Because of the bushes and trees which grow up to the fence it is impossible to see anything of the views without entering the station. As this is not manned constantly anyone who wishes to avoid a disappointing climb must make prior arrangements to enter it. This can be done through the head office of Cable & Wireless at Clare Hall on the eastern outskirts of St John's (telephone 462-0840). The summit is about two and a half miles from the main road. It can only be reached by walking or in a vehicle with four wheel drive. Although the road is well-surfaced for most of its length it is extremely steep in places.

A visit to the top of Boggy Peak is strongly recommended. From it, at just over 1300 feet above sea level, the whole of Antigua (with the exception of small areas hidden by the nearer hills to the south-west and south-east) can be seen. At the same time, with reasonable conditions of visibility, the islands of Guadeloupe, Montserrat, Redonda, Nevis, St Kitts and Barbuda can also be seen quite clearly.

The west coast

From Boggy Peak the full extent of **Cades Reef**, off the coast immediately to the south, can be determined. Further views of it are obtained from the main road as it rounds Johnsons Point. About a mile further on from this point is the splendid beach of Picartes Bay (always known locally as '**Dark Wood**'). This has plenty of shady trees and an adjacent beach bar. Another two miles on is the **Jolly Beach Hotel** on Lignumvitae Bay. This hotel is by far the largest in Antigua. It stretches along one of the best beaches, which is nearly one mile long. The hotel has extensive facilities for water sports, its own windsurfing school, and numerous sailing and fishing boats. There are also regular day tours by boat to Great Bird Island.

The westernmost point of Antigua is called **Pearns Point**. It can be reached by means of a track from Jennings. This village is about two miles from the Jolly Beach Hotel towards St John's. The track is in poor condition and only suitable for cross-country vehicles. It leads to **Hermitage Bay** on the southern side of Five Islands Harbour. This has a fine beach, with calm water and huge numbers of interesting seashells. From Hermitage Bay it is possible to walk to Pearns Point. The five tiny islets which have given Five Islands Harbour its name are just off the Point.

Green Castle Hill

For anyone who enjoys hill-climbing there is a third hill, ranking after Boggy Peak and Monks Hill, which is worth visiting for the view from the top. This is **Green Castle Hill**, which stands by itself at the northern end of the mountainous south-western region. It is about a mile inland from the main road between Jennings and St John's, and about the same distance to the west of the village of Emanuel. A stone quarry is worked on one side of the hill. The track leading to the top, and which is easy to follow, starts near the gates of a brick factory associated with the quarry. The climb is relatively easy and takes about thirty to forty-five minutes, depending on the age and fitness of the climber. From the summit the view to the north is magnificent – and much better than the fairly low elevation of 565 feet and the hill's unprepossessing appearance from the road might lead one to believe.

The ashes of Lord Baldwin, who was Governor of the Leeward Islands from 1947 to 1949, are interred under a large stone plaque at one end of the summit. He helped to bring about much-needed changes in the social life of Antigua during his short tenure of office, and is remembered with affection by many of the older citizens. That this affection was returned is borne out by the words on the plaque, 'He loved the people of these islands'.

On the south and west sides of the hill near the top are some rock pillars and large boulders. As these are in vaguely circular or semi-circular formations they have acquired the reputation of being megaliths set up, as a current tourist brochure would have it, 'by human hands for the worship of the Sun God and the Moon Goddess'. As the pre-Columbian inhabitants of the island practised a form of Nature-worship, with gods of minute proportions, this seems highly unlikely. There is no record of megaliths or their like in any other West Indian island, so it is difficult to believe that Antigua was once inhabited by a race capable of, or indeed wishing to, erect stone columns weighing many tons on top of a hill. The 'megaliths' are undoubtedly of natural formation, of more interest to the geologist than the archaeologist. Green Castle Hill is still worth climbing nevertheless.

Hawks Bill Rock, Deep Bay and Sandy Island

The large peninsula which forms the northern side of Five Islands Harbour can only be reached by a road running west from St John's. This crosses the head of the large marshy area called The Flashes and leads to Five Islands Village. From there it is possible to drive to most of the small bays on the western side of the peninsula. **Hawks Bill Bay**, in the centre, takes its name from the large rock about three hundred yards offshore. From certain directions this looks very much like the head of a hawksbill turtle, a species common in Antiguan waters. Both Hawks Bill Bay and **Galley Bay** immediately to the north have attractive hotels.

The northernmost bay, called **Deep Bay**, is easily the most popular. It is the site of the **Royal Antiguan Hotel**, and there are other resorts and condominium developments in the vicinity. In 1988 a causeway was being built across the inner part of St John's harbour to carry a road which will provide direct access to these developments from the city. The bay is similar in size and shape, but facing in the opposite direction, to Half Moon Bay on the south-east coast. Besides offering equally fine swimming and snorkeling it has the added attraction of a wreck lying in its entrance. This is the steel-hulled barque *Andes* which sank in 1905, while trying to unload a cargo of barrels of pitch, some of which had caught fire. The outline of the vessel can be seen quite clearly a few feet below the surface and the stump of one mast is visible above water. As it lies in less than thirty feet of water it is readily accessible to snorkelers and scuba-divers.

Surf riding at Hawks Bill Beach. The small rollers make it ideal for beginners

Directly to the west of Deep Bay, about two and a half miles offshore, is **Sandy Island**. This is only a few feet high and, apart from one or two bushes and a navigation light, is deserted. Just to the south-west of it is Weymouth Reef. This was named after the British frigate *HMS Weymouth* which was wrecked there in 1745. The wreck which can be seen there today is an Antiguan coaster. As if trying to demonstrate that there had been no advance in navigational competence in the intervening 239 years, this went aground in exactly the same place in 1984.

Fort Barrington

The northern side of Deep Bay is formed by **Goat Hill**, which is the site of the fort built to protect the outer entrance to St John's Harbour. The hill was fortified from the earliest days of the settlement and has seen more action than any other fort in the island (which of course, for anyone who has read so far, is not saying a great deal ...). It was the first place captured by the French when they occupied Antigua from November 1666 until July 1667. The present fortifications were not built until 1779. They were named **Fort Barrington** in honour of the British admiral who had captured the island of St Lucia from the French the year before. Needless to say, once it had been built the fort saw no enemy action. After the end of the Napoleonic wars it became little more than a signal station, signalling the approach of ships to another station on Rat Island in the inner harbour.

The fort is reached by a track which winds up Goat Hill from the northern end of the beach in Deep Bay. About halfway up it passes a small abandoned building. This had nothing to do with the fort but was erected much later. It used to house equipment connected with an underwater telephone cable which terminated in Deep Bay many years ago. The climb is easy and takes about fifteen minutes. It is well worthwhile and provides a most satisfactory closure of a traverse of the island begun at Fort James, a mile away on the opposite side of the harbour.

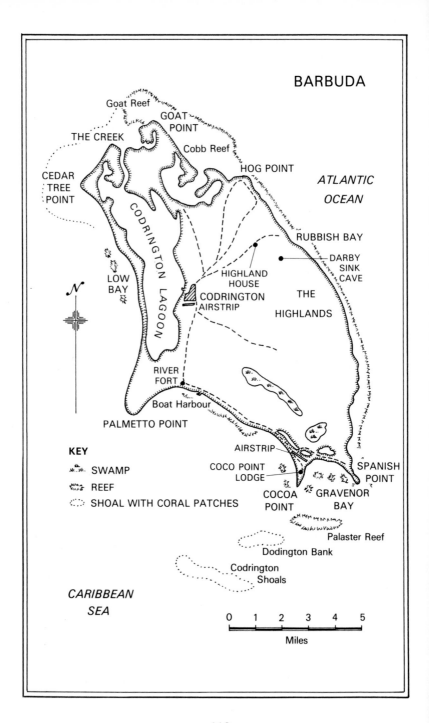

BARBUDA

Goat Reef

GOAT POINT

THE CREEK

Cobb Reef

CEDAR TREE POINT

HOG POINT

ATLANTIC OCEAN

RUBBISH BAY

DARBY SINK CAVE

CODRINGTON LAGOON

LOW BAY

HIGHLAND HOUSE

CODRINGTON AIRSTRIP

THE HIGHLANDS

N

RIVER FORT

Boat Harbour

PALMETTO POINT

AIRSTRIP

COCO POINT LODGE

COCOA POINT

SPANISH POINT

GRAVENOR BAY

KEY

SWAMP

REEF

SHOAL WITH CORAL PATCHES

Palaster Reef

Dodington Bank

Codrington Shoals

CARIBBEAN SEA

0 1 2 3 4 5

Miles

118

Chapter thirteen

Barbuda and Redonda

Barbuda cannot be seen from Antigua, unless a special effort to see it is made by climbing Boggy Peak. On the other hand, Antigua can be seen clearly from Barbuda under most conditions of visibility. This situation well sums up the relationship between the two islands. Barbuda has always been a 'poor relation' of Antigua: Antiguans are unaware of its existence for most of the time, while Barbudans – who depend on Antigua for almost their every need – must be reminded frequently of their dependency.

Formation

Barbuda is about seventy square miles in extent if the large lagoon on the western side is included in the total area. Two-thirds of the island consists of an almost flat plain raised only a few feet above sea level. The other third, known as The Highlands, is a flat tableland which has a maximum height of 128 feet. The whole island is limestone and represents a coral reef which was raised above the sea in two successive stages. The Highlands form steep cliffs on the eastern, windward, side, otherwise the whole island is devoid of any natural features which can be identified from seaward. The island has even less rainfall than Antigua, and there are no streams or lakes. Fortunately underground water is found in reasonable quantities and is obtained from wells. Virtually the whole coastline is fringed with coral reefs. Throughout its history Barbuda has been an exceptionally dangerous hazard to shipping.

119

History

The history of Barbuda is unlike that of any other West Indian island. Very little is known about its discovery, reconnaissance and early European settlement. Even the origin of its name is obscure. The Spanish certainly knew of its existence in the early 16th century, but the first recorded attempt at settling was made by an Englishman in 1628. This failed because of attacks by Caribs and because the island was 'so barren'. The true history begins later in the 17th century when two other Englishmen, Christopher and John Codrington, leased the whole island from the British Crown for a peppercorn rent variously recorded as 'one Fat Sheep (if demanded)', 'one sufficient Able horse', a turtle or a buck.

Because of the indifferent soil and poor rainfall the plantation system was never developed in Barbuda. Consequently its population was unlike that of Antigua or any other plantation island. Slaves were imported by the Codringtons to raise crops and to look after cattle and other animals which were also imported. By the middle of the 18th century the mainstay of the economy was game and livestock. About two hundred slaves grew ground provisions, fished, caught turtles, cut firewood and from time to time salvaged wrecks. None of the Codrington family lived in the island permanently, and for most of the time the slaves were only casually supervised by one or two white overseers. With the freedom to grow their own provisions, with access to a great amount of livestock, and living in a dry healthy climate, the slaves enjoyed much better circumstances than those in the plantation islands.

It is a widely held belief that the large stature of many Barbudans is due to the Codringtons having used the island as a slave-breeding 'nursery'. This has been proved conclusively to be a myth, based on a mis-reading of a fragment of the documentary history of the Codrington family. Any genetic tendency towards great height and build is far more likely to be due to generations of Barbudans having enjoyed an abundance of protein from fish and livestock, while living relatively stress-free lives in a salubrious climate.

By all accounts emancipation in 1834 made little difference to the way of life or standard of living in Barbuda. The Barbudans showed much unwillingness to leave the island as slaves – faced with the prospect of work on a plantation in Antigua or elsewhere – and just as little inclination to leave once they were free. Those who did leave after 1834 were, in the main, forced to do so because no employment was offered to them on what was still a private estate. For those that remained, perhaps five hundred in all, life continued much as before.

The Codrington family continued to lease the island until as late as 1870, although Barbuda had been formally annexed to Antigua ten years earlier. After the Codringtons, others tried to 'govern by lease', without any success, until the end of the century. In 1903 the island was declared to be a Crown Estate and the authorities in Antigua were ordered to run it as such. The position of Warden was established and this official effectively administered the island for the next three-quarters of a century. In 1976 the Warden was replaced by the Barbuda Council. This body has no less than nine elected and two *ex officio* members, with sufficient powers to make the island virtually self-governing. While it would be inappropriate, to say the least, to describe Barbuda as the Athens of the Caribbean, the relatively enormous size of this Council (with an elector-elected ratio of about seventy to one) means that the internal affairs of the island are conducted in a fashion approaching the Athenian ideal, and emulated in few other parts of the world. Whether of course the island's affairs are handled any more efficiently than they were in the hands of the solitary Warden, is something about which the six hundred or so registered voters probably have six hundred or more different views.

Economy

The economy of Barbuda, which after emancipation had depended to a large extent on the 'wrecking' industry and subsistence farming, today depends on fishing, subsistence farming, tourism and, as in Antigua, the 'hidden factor'. There are probably at least six times as many Barbudans living abroad as on

The village of Codrington

the island. Their remittances form a substantial part of the total income. Two hundred years ago the island had one village called, not suprisingly, Codrington, and about three hundred acres under cultivation. The rest of the island was wild and overgrown with bush, in which roamed large numbers of sheep, goats, cattle, horses, pigs, mules and deer. And this is very much as the island remains today, with perhaps slightly fewer acres under cultivation and the animal population severely reduced. **Codrington** remains the only village, still housing the entire population of probably no more than a thousand. The modern additions consist of little more than two air-strips (one near the village and the other near the island's single beach hotel in the south-east), a small and very basic boat harbour on the south coast, and thirty to forty motor vehicles. There is also an electricity generating plant and a small cottage hospital.

Places of interest

In spite of the apparent lack of change, or possibly because of the air of timelessness, Barbuda does have its attractions. This is particularly so for anyone interested in the simpler pleasures and more pastoral activities. For those who enjoy walking, horseback riding, bird-watching, shelling and beachcombing, caving, camping, or just observing animal and plant life, Barbuda has much to offer. For others who want to indulge in less peaceful activities it also provides facilities for deer-hunting, duck-shooting and deep sea fishing.

The beaches are even better than those of Antigua. The ones on the south and west coasts are each several miles in length, and for most of the time utterly deserted. The small beaches on the north-eastern side (about four miles from Codrington) between the two geographic features with the unfortunate names of **Rubbish Bay** and **Hog Point** are equally fine, and hold an added attraction. Facing a three thousand mile expanse of ocean these beaches receive flotsam originating anywhere in the North Atlantic as well as from Western Europe and West Africa. They provide some of the best beachcombing in the Caribbean. Offshore, enormous stretches of coral reef surround the island on three sides. With their abundance of marine life and the remains of several centuries worth of wrecks, they provide plenty of interest for the snorkeling or diving enthusiast.

As is to be expected in an island composed of limestone Barbuda has numerous caves and the surface of The Highlands is littered with sink holes. Probably the most interesting is **Darby Sink Cave**, about three and a half miles north-east of Codrington. This is the largest sink hole, about a hundred yards in diameter and around eighty feet deep, with a reasonably easy descent to the bottom. The Highlands cave system is virtually unexplored and certainly unmapped. While stories of underground lakes, sightless fresh water shrimps and prehistoric rock carvings in some of the caves need to be treated with some scepticism, there is no doubt that there is a lot to attract visitors interested in speleology or pot-holing.

It is not suprising, considering its peculiar history, that Barbuda has very few historic sites. Evidence has been found here and there of prehistoric occupation, but nothing remains that is of interest to anyone other than the professional or committed amateur archaeologist. Of the various historic structures scattered around the island only two warrant the visitor making the effort to view them. The ruins of **Highland House**, the Codrington family's residence near the highest part of the island, are worth visiting. They are on the north-western shoulder of The Highlands, about three miles from Codrington. The house was built around 1750, but as it was never occupied permanently it remained standing for no more than fifty or sixty years. Today all that remain are the floors and lower walls, and a large cistern, almost entirely overgrown. Perhaps the biggest attraction of a visit is the wonderful view of the island which can be obtained in every direction except to the south.

What is popularly called **'River Fort'** is the most impressive structure on the island. This is a Martello Tower and a raised gun platform situated on the south coast overlooking what used to be the main landing place, called The River. The reason for this choice of name is unclear; there never has been a river here or anywhere else in Barbuda. The fort was probably built in the early part of the 19th century when this type of fortification (modelled on a tower built on Cape Mortella in Corsica which proved exceptionally difficult to capture during the Napoleonic wars) became popular in British military engineering circles. It has extremely thick walls and the whole structure, considering the size and importance of Barbuda, was built on a monumental scale. Like many similar structures still found around the coasts of England, River Fort never saw or heard a shot fired in anger. Probably its most useful function, which continues to the present, was to act as a conspicuous landmark for vessels approaching from the south. It is about three miles from Codrington, and reached by the main road out of the village.

Visitors should beware of making too much of **'The Castle'** shown on maps of the island near Spanish Point in the south-east. This is a misnomer for the ruins of a small stone lookout and storage building. It was probably built in the 18th century but has long since fallen into disrepair. Similarly, the ruins of another building at the base of **Gun Shop Cliff** to the east of Highland House have nothing at all to do with the siting or manufacturing of guns. This structure was erected in the late 19th century as part of a short-lived phosphate mining operation, which took place inside one of the caves which penetrate the cliffs in this area.

Travel arrangements

Having mentioned some of the island's attractions it has to be pointed out that there is very little to be found in the way of facilities, support or provisions for any sort of outdoor activity requiring specialist equipment – be it a tent, an air bottle, or even a torch or a map. This may well add to Barbuda's attraction for the visitor who wants to indulge in some form of activity other than swimming, sunbathing and snorkeling. Much of the, for example, speleologist's or scuba-diver's satisfaction probably stems from having to rely mainly on his own planning, resources and initiative while indulging in his particular pastime. But, special equipment and facilities apart, the speleologist, scuba-diver or anyone else intending to pay a visit (other than as a guest at Coco Point Lodge, for whom private arrangements are made) should arrange the visit through a travel agent in Antigua. Everyone has to arrive in Antigua first in any case. There are no flights to Barbuda from anywhere else in the world. There are several agents in St John's who specialise in arranging such visits. A one-day conducted tour is available at short notice, but longer stays can be organised to suit individual requirements. Barbuda is linked by telephone to Antigua and an internal telephone system was introduced in 1986. There is no public transport but enough vehicles are available for rent to enable visitors to tour the island. Accommodation in Codrington is limited to one small hotel, a few cottages and one or two apartments. Accordingly all arrangements for accommodation and transport must be made well in advance.

The island is about twenty minutes' flying time away from Antigua. There are two scheduled return flights daily by LIAT, using twin-engined 'Islander' aircraft. Charter flights are flown in similar or smaller aircraft as required. All flights use the Codrington airstrip, other than those with guests for the exclusive beach hotel, Coco Point Lodge, which has its own landing field.

There is no regular, scheduled or organised communication by sea between Antigua and Barbuda. A number of small auxillary-powered sailing vessels trade between the two islands, and these will carry passengers on the odd occasion. All arrangements to take passage need to be made with the captain of the vessel

Coco Point Lodge and Gravenor Bay

concerned. This will necessitate the prospective passenger first of all locating a suitable craft in St John's Harbour. It is not possible here to give any guidance on how this can be done, other than by making verbal enquiries at the waterfront. Most of the vessels unload at a small wharf inside the little harbour on the south coast of Barbuda, about half a mile east of River Fort. The only alternative is a small pier at Codrington, reached through a narrow passage at the northern end of the lagoon. The prospective passenger will need to find out before sailing which destination is intended. The sea crossing itself, given the size and condition of most of the craft, cannot fail to be an exciting and memorable experience. It is not recommended for the over-fastidious, nor for the traveller unsure of her sea legs.

Redonda

Redonda

The third and by far the smallest part of the State of Antigua and Barbuda is the rocky, uninhabited island of **Redonda**. It is just over thirty miles away from the nearest point of Antigua, and roughly halfway between Montserrat and Nevis. It is about one mile long north to south and less than half a mile wide. It rises to nearly 1000 feet above the sea with steep cliffs on all sides. It was sighted by Columbus on the same day that he discovered Antigua. He gave it the name **Santa Maria la Redonda** (St Mary the Round), displacing another disagreeable Carib appellation, Ocanamunru, with one that was both apt and melodious.

The first recorded landing took place in 1687, but it was not until well into the 19th century that anyone took any interest in it. Phosphate in bird guano was found in commercially viable quantities and a mining operation was begun by a US firm in the 1860s. This led to Redonda being annexed to Antigua in 1869. The mining was done by labourers hired mainly from Montserrat, which is only about thirteen miles away. It continued until about 1920, although nothing was shipped from the island after the outbreak of the First World War. At its height production was from 3000 to 4000 tons of phosphate a year. The output declined steadily after reaching a peak in 1895. The mining company relinquished its lease in 1930 and Redonda has been unoccupied ever since. It is visited from time to time by yachtsmen, but otherwise its only inhabitants are goats, rats, crabs and numerous seabirds.

In 1865 while sailing past Redonda, and with no authority other than his native Irish eccentricity, a certain Matthew Shiell decided to claim it as a 'fiefdom' for his son. Matthew Phipps Shiell, the son, was given the title of 'King Phillipe I' by his father, and he subsequently bequeathed his 'fiefdom' to a minor English poet, who styled himself 'King Juan I'. A number of 'dukes' and 'duchesses' of Redonda were created by Juan I, and he later appointed as his successor another Englishman, who now calls himself 'King Juan II'.

Any humour attached to all this claptrap must surely have died with the second Matthew Shiell, if not the first (a large rock covered with the accumulated birddroppings of countless millenia is not, after all, the finest of birthrights . . .). Regardless of this the harmless charade continues to the present day (probably kept alive only by references such as this – given here only because the story is widely known and the unwary might believe the claim had some validity), and the 'king' is known to have visited his 'fiefdom' in recent years. One can only hope that his dignity was not too upset by his having to produce a passport in Antigua before setting off to Redonda, and that he filled in his immigration form correctly . . .

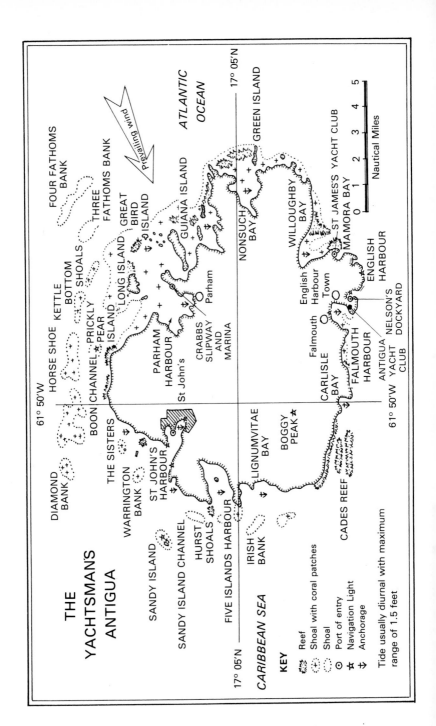

THE
YACHTSMAN'S
ANTIGUA

17° 05'N

CARIBBEAN SEA

KEY

Reef
Shoal with coral patches
Shoal
Port of entry
Navigation Light
Anchorage

Tide usually diurnal with maximum
range of 1.5 feet

DIAMOND
BANK

SANDY ISLAND

SANDY ISLAND CHANNEL

HURST
SHOALS

FIVE ISLANDS HARBOUR

IRISH
BANK

WARRINGTON
BANK

THE SISTERS

ST JOHN'S
HARBOUR

LIGNUMVITAE
BAY

BOGGY
PEAK

CADES REEF

61° 50'W

HORSE SHOE KETTLE

BOTTOM
SHOALS

PRICKLY
PEAR
ISLAND

BOON CHANNEL

PARHAM
HARBOUR

St John's

CRABBS
SLIPWAY
AND
MARINA

Parham

LONG ISLAND

GREAT
BIRD
ISLAND

GUIANA ISLAND

NONSUCH
BAY

CARLISLE
BAY

Falmouth

FALMOUTH
HARBOUR

ANTIGUA
YACHT
CLUB

English
Harbour
Town

ENGLISH
HARBOUR

NELSON'S
DOCKYARD

WILLOUGHBY
BAY

ST JAMES'S YACHT CLUB

MAMORA BAY

FOUR FATHOMS
BANK

THREE
FATHOMS BANK

Prevailing wind

ATLANTIC
OCEAN

17° 05'N

GREEN ISLAND

61° 50'W

Nautical Miles

0   1   2   3   4   5

Chapter fourteen

Sailing in Antigua and Barbuda

No guide to Antigua and Barbuda could be complete without some information on the islands' attractions and facilities for visiting yachtsmen. English Harbour has been a favourite port of call for ocean-going yachts since the end of the Second World War, but the true potential of the waters around the islands only began to be realised from the mid-1960s. Since then sailing in general, and ocean cruising in particular, have increased enormously in popularity. In 1960 it is doubtful if more than a hundred yachts visited Antigua in a year. By 1970 English Harbour alone was recording more than six hundred arrivals each year, and by 1980 the figure had risen to over two thousand. The services available for yachtsmen increased accordingly, and today Antigua has some of the best yachting facilities in the Caribbean.

The start of the race

Antigua is directly on the traditional trade wind sailing route from Europe to the West Indies. It is one of the prime landfalls, especially for boats making for the Pacific through the Panama Canal. It is in the middle of the Leeward Islands, within sight of Guadeloupe, Montserrat and Nevis, and so provides a good base for cruising in that area. The weather conditions during the main cruising season from mid-November to mid-May are generally ideal. The trade wind blows from between north-east and south-east at between ten and twenty knots. Fog and gales are unknown. There is no tidal range to speak of, and the ocean current flows in a steady westerly direction at an average rate of about fifteen nautical miles a day. While the inshore waters around both Antigua and Barbuda are littered with hazards in the form of coral heads, patches and reefs there are few which cannot be seen clearly from a boat under normal light conditions. There are sufficient stretches of open and enclosed water, with passages and anchorages of every kind, to provide enjoyable sailing for everyone from the most inexperienced weekend sailor to the most travelled sunburnt shellback.

Entry formalities

The skipper of any yacht visiting Antigua must complete a Port Authority Clearance Form and produce clearance papers from his last port of call. Each member of the crew must have a valid passport or, in the case of US or Canadian citizens, some other official proof of identity. The Immigration and Customs officials are by now well used to dealing with yachtsmen, whom they expect to obey the rules and to follow the correct procedures. A crew member is not allowed to transfer to another yacht unless the boat to which he is moving is about to leave. Anyone leaving a yacht for any other reason must have a valid airline ticket to another destination, which it is the skipper's responsibility to provide. Medical drugs and firearms must be declared. Every boat in the waters of the State must carry a valid cruising permit, issued for one month and renewable. Outward clearance is normally given only on the day of departure, after payment of the appropriate harbour dues.

Ports of entry

To facilitate the entry of yachts there are now four ports of entry in Antigua. There is also one in Barbuda, but before going there a yacht must be cleared in Antigua and the necessary cruising permit obtained.

St John's Harbour   Although the Deep Water Port is solely for the use of commercial shipping, the inner harbour between the dredged turning basin and the Treasury Pier offers an excellent anchorage for yachts. There are no fees payable for using this anchorage. St John's provides by far the widest range of shopping at the cheapest prices, particularly for fresh fruit and vegetables. Fresh water, fuel and ice are all easy to obtain. There are no repair, maintenance or alongside berthing facilities.

Crabbs Slipway and Marina   This is a privately owned concern on the western side of Crabbs Peninsula on the north coast. It consists of a boat yard with a fifty-ton travel lift, general maintenance facilities and alongside berths for about thirty boats. There is also a chandlery, laundry, restaurant, gift shop, post office and showers. There are also some small 'efficiency apartments' and storage rooms. The marina houses a 'bareboat' yacht chartering operation. Parham, the nearest village and from where there is a bus service into St John's, is about two miles away.

St James's Yacht Club   The facilities of this club in Mamora Bay on the south-east coast are reserved for the use of boats owned or skippered by members of the St James's Club. There is alongside berthing for up to thirty boats, a workshop, chandlery, laundry, showers and a restaurant. The bay provides anchorage room for up to one hundred yachts.

English Harbour   This is the main port of entry for yachts. It has been developed over the years to provide every service and facility needed by yachtsmen. Alongside berths are available at the Dockyard Quay and there is good anchorage throughout the harbour. Between November and May the harbour is very busy and it may be difficult sometimes to find room to anchor safely. Within the Dockyard there are showers, lockers, a sailmaker, a marine electronics repair shop, gift shops and a restaurant. On the opposite side of the harbour there is a slipway which can handle craft up to one hundred feet in length, together with an engineering workshop and a large chandlery. There is also an alongside berth where fuel and water can be embarked. Postal, banking and overseas telephone services are available in the large building just outside the Dockyard gate. Between this building and English Harbour Town there are groceries, repair shops, several eating places and a laundry. English Harbour is the centre in Antigua for yacht chartering. A considerable number of yachts, with or without crews, are available for every type of sailing vacation or expedition.

The facilities of the Dockyard and its environs are equally accessible to yachts moored in **Falmouth Harbour**. This is used increasingly as an overflow from English Harbour. It is not a port of entry and clearance has to be obtained in English Harbour before using it. The most popular area for anchoring is off the Antigua Yacht Club which is a quarter of a mile to the west of the isthmus separating the two harbours. Practically on the isthmus itself is a Port Authority office, a fuel and water jetty and a building with public showers. An alternative berth is provided on the north side of Falmouth Harbour at the catamaran marina. This can accommodate twenty boats alongside. Its facilities include fuel, water, showers, storerooms and a small chandlery.

It is appropriate here to add a word of caution. While it is impossible to dispute the primacy of English Harbour's facilities and attractions for yachtsmen, it is equally impossible to consider it in any way representative of the remainder of Antigua. The way and pace of life, the casual dress (and sometimes equally casual behaviour), and the general standard of living of most of the visiting yachtsmen, are not common to the rest of the island. These factors, combined with the activities of the disproportionate number of non-nationals who live and work in the area, give English Harbour a special and very different ambience. Yachting and sailing are not pastimes which appeal to, or are within the reach of, more than a tiny minority of Antiguans. In and around English Harbour Antiguans, and particularly black Antiguans, remain in the background filling subordinate positions. The visiting yachtsman who throughout his stay keeps his boat in English Harbour or Falmouth Harbour, will not on his departure be able to claim with any great conviction that he has seen

Antigua or knows much about the people – any more than the vacationer who spends all his time in and around his hotel.

Cruising

The coastline of Antigua, if that of the off-lying islands is included, is well over ninety miles in length. It affords intriguing problems of navigation and seamanship, splendid sailing with superb views, dozens of secluded anchorages, and plenty of landing places. While the island has possibly more than its fair share of coral reefs these present little danger – provided the proper seamanlike precautions are taken. Those some distance off the coast protect the shoreline and ensure reasonably calm conditions in the bays and inshore passages. The reefs are also largely responsible for the white sandy beaches which add to the attraction of most of the coves which contain the best anchorages.

It goes without saying that it is dangerous to sail around the island without up-to-date charts and pilotage information. Great Britain remains the charting authority for all of the former British colonies in the Caribbean. British charts of Antigua (upon which those published by any other country are based) provide the most authentic representation of the coastline and inshore waters. Charts produced by commercial publishers, based on the official ones and purporting to show additional information, should be treated with some reserve. The 'new' details are often of dubious authenticity or of little practical value to the stranger entering Antiguan waters for the first time. The use of larger scales to show the same information charted on the official charts at a smaller scale in no way improves the accuracy of commercial 'yachting' charts. Of more value are the various yachting guides and handbooks which are available. These give detailed information about the facilities available in each port of entry, together with sailing directions for the more popular cruising areas and anchorages. It is still necessary to recognise that, by virtue of the way these books are compiled and the length of time they remain in print, they will contain much that is outdated, misleading or totally bogus. The yachtsman who will get the most satisfaction and enjoyment from cruising in Antiguan waters is the one who uses such publications merely to supplement his own judgement, experience and capability.

Compared with many other islands in the eastern Caribbean, Antigua has a reasonable number of navigational aids in the form of lights, buoys, leading marks and a radio direction-finding beacon. Although there are leading lights marking the entrances into St John's, Falmouth and English harbours, it is not recommended that any of these be entered at night, unless in an emergency. The waters inside each harbour are too encumbered with natural and man-made hazards to permit safe manoeuvring in the dark.

While in Antiguan waters, regardless of the time of year, all professional yachtsmen will monitor local weather forecasts as a matter of course. The season for cruising in the Caribbean is between November and May, because this is the period during which hurricanes are least likely. However records show that a severe storm can occur in any month of the year – the 'hurricane season' from July to October being only the period when they are most likely. The possibility of such a storm hitting Antigua in, say, December or May is extremely remote. Nevertheless, the yacht owner or skipper who has a contingency plan ready to put into effect at any time during his stay in Antiguan waters will be the one who enjoys the greatest peace of mind.

Barbuda

As a cruising area the waters of Barbuda are not recommended for the novice. To begin with, although the island is only about twenty-five nautical miles north of Antigua it is not that easy to find. Most of it is only a few feet above sea level and it is necessary to approach within two or three miles before anything is seen. The North Equatorial Current which flows across the bank between the two islands has a rate which is unpredictable from season to season. If insufficient allowance is made for the current the west coast of Barbuda can be missed completely; if too much allowance is made a boat can end up amidst the reefs off the south-east coast. The only two features of navigational significance are the Martello tower near the south-west corner and Coco Point Lodge, the hotel on Cocoa Point in the south-east. It is essential to plan to make a landfall around midday with the sun as high overhead as possible. All the reefs can then be seen. The waters between the two islands are fished extensively, and well sprinkled with fishermens' floats. These can be made of plastic, glass, fibreglass or wood, and they are often difficult to see from any great distance. They provide another good reason for making the crossing only in daylight.

Most yachts use **Gravenor Bay**, between Cocoa Point and Spanish Point in the south-east, as an anchorage. This provides plenty of shelter, excellent fishing and snorkeling, and ready access to the wild eastern coast of the island. **Palaster Reef**, about two miles offshore to the south of the bay, is a protected area. No fishing or interference with the reef or its marine life is allowed. This reef is only one of many all around the island which have been responsible for the large number of wrecks recorded in Barbuda's history. The various yachting guides make great play with this, and give the impression that many of the wrecks are readily seen when diving or snorkeling. Unfortunately this is not the case. While the names and circumstances of many losses are recorded, the positions in which they went aground or sank are known only very approximately. Any map or chart giving precise positions of named wrecks will, regrettably, be found to be quite bogus. Anyone keen on underwater exploration may well come across some evidence of a wreck, but it is most unlikely that any identification will be possible.

Codrington village on the eastern side of the lagoon is not normally visited by yachts. The only entrance to the lagoon is through a tortuous shallow channel at the northern end. In any case Codrington has no facilities or services for yachts. The attractions of Barbuda are mentioned in Chapter 13, and many will appeal to yachtsmen as much as to the general sightseer or tourist. Indeed yachtsmen form a significant proportion of the total of all visitors to the island each year. For the skipper and crew who really want to 'get away from it all' – to have a calm anchorage and miles of deserted white beach all to themselves, and to be able to swim in water totally free from the flotsam and debris of modern civilisation – Barbuda is *the* place. But, like anyone else indulging in a pastime in Barbuda which requires specialist gear and facilities, the crew of a yacht must be entirely self-sufficient. The sagacious skipper will be ever conscious that an incident such as a grounding – which would be serious enough in Antigua where there are rescue, salvage and repair facilities available – may well mean total disaster off Barbuda, where there are none of these facilities.

Redonda

Should any yachtsman wish to risk the displeasure of 'King Juan II' of Redonda (perhaps a figure to rank with Calypso, Circe and the Cyclopes in the demonology of the ocean voyager) a landing may be made on that island in favourable sea conditions. The only anchorage is off the south-western corner, but the holding ground is poor and there is very little shelter from the prevailing wind and swell. No respectable skipper would wish to risk his boat for more than a few hours, and this is all that is required to view the island.

Windsurfing and waterskiing from Hawks Bill Beach

Sailing week, Antigua

Windsurfing

The normal weather and sea conditions make the inshore waters of Antigua ideal for board sailing. In recent years this sport has become firmly established. There are now three International Windsurfer Sailing Schools and various other sailing centres attached to some of the larger hotels. A number of board sailing events are held each year, including **Windsurfing Antigua Week** in April. These attract local and visiting participants, with every degree of skill. With all the right conditions for beginners along the leeward side of the island, and the exciting wind and sea conditions off the less sheltered coasts which appeal to the more professional, Antigua has much to offer all windsurfing enthusiasts.

139

Antigua Sailing Week

Each year since 1968 the Antigua Hotel Association has organised a special programme of yacht races during the last week in April. This event has now become one of the finest ocean racing events in the world. Each year it attracts more and more entrants. It is an international event with yachts from perhaps twenty different countries racing in six or seven different classes under the International Yacht Racing Rules. The programme consists of five races, including one over an Olympic course, spread over seven days. It is preceded by two passage races, one from Antigua around Montserrat and Redonda, and the other from Guadeloupe to Antigua. All the racing is extremely competitive but Sailing Week has an enviable reputation for putting the accent on 'fair sailing' and the pleasure of taking part in such splendid sea and weather conditions.

The mid-week 'lay day' is given over to more light-hearted events centred on the Antigua Yacht Club in Falmouth Harbour. These include a single-handed race, a water carnival, a nautical tug-of-war and a rubber raft race. The final day of Sailing Week is also devoted to fun and games, at the Dockyard in English Harbour. There the activities attract not only the racing crews and visiting yachtsmen, but also the general public. The main attraction is the non-mariners' race, using engineless craft which have not cost more than EC$100 to build, and which have never been in the water before the race begins. This is accompanied by, as the official Sailing Week programme puts it succinctly every year, 'general hellraising'. The day, and Sailing Week as a whole, ends with prize-giving by the Governor-General, a marching display by the Royal Antigua Police Force, and a dance called, inevitably as it is held in the Dockyard, 'The Lord Nelson's Ball'.

Sailing Week is organised and run in a very professional manner and deserves its place among the premier ocean racing events in the world. Besides its obvious appeal to the professional yacht-racing fraternity and yachtsmen in general, it has much to attract the less nautically inclined visitor. The events of the two 'lay days' speak for themselves. Much of the activity concerned with the actual races takes place in the approaches to English and Falmouth harbours, and close inshore along the south and west coasts.

Armed with a copy of the official programme, which is free and widely distributed in the island, the interested visitor will be able to follow the races from suitable viewing points around the coast. More information about Sailing Week can be obtained from:

The Secretary
Antigua Sailing Week
Antigua Yacht Club
English Harbour
Antigua
Tel: 462-1444

Envoi

With Antigua as the key link in a chain of islands separating the Caribbean Sea from the enormity of the Atlantic Ocean it goes without saying that the sea has played a vital role throughout the island's history. The importance of the sea and ships to Antigua is just as great today as when the first Arawak canoe grounded on one of its beaches, or when Columbus sighted it from somewhere north of Montserrat nearly five hundred years ago. While I imagine that very few of the yachtsmen who visit Antigua each year would think of themselves as in any way following in the wake of Columbus, it is worth remembering that the sea remains exactly as it was in his day and that, regardless of advances in techniques, boat design, materials and aids to navigation, sailing to Antigua still depends on the same North-East Trade Wind.

It seems, to me at least, highly appropriate that sailing vessels – albeit mostly in the form of expensive yachts intended for pleasure – are still found in Antiguan waters and in increasing numbers. It is equally appropriate that sailing, in the form of the revenue derived from the yachting industry, continues to make a sizeable contribution to the economic development of the State.

Some Antiguan proverbs

The following selection of local proverbs is taken from the extensive collection made by Mrs O E Henry, of Cochrane's House, Cochranes, Antigua. While some of them may also be found in other West Indian islands, perhaps in a slightly different form, they are all in current use among Antiguans.

A good kip [kept woman] better than a bad marriage.
Absence of body better than presence of mind.
Better man belly bus' than good food waste.
Cockroach ha' no right in fowl house.
Com-com-sah [to curry favour] worse than obeah.
Come see me is one t'ing; come live with me is another.
De worse o' livin' better than de bes' o' dead.
Don't talk cattle on cattle back.
Empty bag can't stand.
Every day bucket go to well; one day rope mus' cut.
Every dog is lion in he own backyard.
Furder [further] in de copse better de shady [shade].
Fre'n' in court better than money in pocket.
God pay debt widdout money.
Guinea bird keep company wid fowl when he foot bruk [broken].
Higher monkey climb de more he show he arse.
If crab na walk he na get fat: if he walk too much he fall in pot.
If you can't be a figure don't be a naught.
If you lie down wid dog you get up wid fleas.
Jackass say dis world ain't level.
Mek sure better than cocksure.

Mout' open – story jump out.

No fisherman ever say he fish stink.

Not for want of tongue why cattle don't talk.

Parson christen he own pickney [children] first.

Play wid puppy, puppy lick yo' mout'; play wid big dog, big dog
bite you.

Rice what bubble in pot lie flat on plate.

Same stick beat wild goat beat tame one.

Ship won't heed to de rudder, rock bound to pick 'im up.

Stan' stiff an' die strong.

Stone under water na know when sun hot.

Tek time, walk fas'.

Two man crab can't live in de same hole.

Walk'bout fool better dan siddown fool.

What come off de hill fall in valley.

What pussy lef' dog well want.

What sweet in de mout' is sour in de belly.

When crab know he back sof' he stop under rock.

When dog mawger [thin and skinny] him head big.

When horse see dead [death] in he eye, he don't care where he
t'row de rider.

When fish come outta sea an' say whale has sore eye an' runny
nose, you believe.

When man dead grass grow at he door.

When t'ief t'ief from t'ief God laugh.

When you go fo' dig one grave, na dig one – dig two.

Why look in de dark wid fire-stick when it ha' broad daylight to
do it?

Wuk [work] older dan you.